Herb *"Tootle"* Estes
The Little Engine That Could

by
Gary L. Parker

WALDENHOUSE PUBLISHERS, INC.
WALDEN, TENNESSEE

Herb"Tootle"Estes: The Little Engine That Could
Copyright ©2016 Gary L. Parker. All rights reserved. No part of this book may be reproduced in any form or by any electronic or mechanical means including information storage and retrieval systems, without permission in writing from the author. The only exception is by a reviewer, who may quote short excerpts in a review.
Front cover art by Kent Harrelson.
Type and design by Karen Paul Stone
ISBN: 978-1-935186-82-3
Published by Waldenhouse Publishers, Inc.
100 Clegg Street, Signal Mountain, Tennessee 37377 USA
888-222-8228   www.waldenhouse.com
Printed in the United States of America
Library of Congress Control Number 2016915147

    "Biography of Herb "Tootle" Estes, Southern auto racing legend. Estes started his career in a midget, then raced jalopies, sportsmans, modifieds, and skeeters. As NASCAR became popular during the 1950's, he drove in every division of that series, ending his career in the popular dirt late models. 164 photographs." -- Provided by Publisher
SPO028000 Sports & Recreation - Motor Sports
SPO019000 Sports & Recreation - History
TRA001050 Transportation: Automotive - History
HIS036120 History: United States - South

Other books by this author:

Red Clay and Dust: The Evolution of Southern Dirt Racing
Copyright 2015© Gary L. Parker ISBN: 978-1-935186-61-8
Library of Congress Control Number: 2015911265

The Rock-em, Sock-em, Travelin' Sideways Dirt Show: A History of Robert Smawley's NDRA
Copyright © 2016 Gary L. Parker. ISBN: 978-1-935186-69-4
Library of Congress Control Number: 2016900468

To order contact the author, Gary L. Parker
1517 Maxwell Road, Chattanooga, TN 37412
423-580-2690 • eparker0923@gmail.com
or go to
www. waldenhouse.com – or –www.amazon.com

DEDICATION

To my wife, Elaine

It was on May 27, 1967 that we started or lives together. On that Saturday night I talked her into going to a dirt race at Smoky Mountain Speedway on our honeymoon. As fate would have it, Tootle Estes, driving the Woody Bradley yellow #28 Ford Fairlane won that race. For years she unselfishly supported me as I worked in the pits with Jody Ridley, H.E. Vineyard, and others. She faithfully traveled with me to hundreds of races all over the country. Now she is with me as I am doing what I should have been doing all along, writing about and promoting the sport that I truly love – Dirt Late Model Racing.

Gary L. Parker

TABLE OF CONTENTS

Herb "Tootle" Estes

ACKNOWLEDGMENTS

For a number of years I had been contemplating writing a book on one of the most unique drivers in Southern racing history, Herbert "Tootle" Estes. One day after visiting his son, Rocky Estes, at his home in Knoxville, Tennessee the book was off and running.

There are a number of people that I owe a special thanks to. First, Rocky Estes who provided me with photos, articles, personal insights, and little known family information about his dad. Also, Tootle's sister, Martha Estes Bodie, provided me with a great family photo and some funny personal stories about her brother.

Another personal friend I can always count on when the going gets tough is the noted writer/racing historian, Bob Markos. Bob provided me with the hard to find information on Estes' NASCAR racing career. He also provided photos, articles, and stats on other areas of Tootle Estes' career.

Just as I was about to give up on finding it my friend, Wayne Wells, provided me with the photo of the yellow #28 Ford Fairlane that I had looked a number years for. He also provided several other great photos and a lot of valuable information on Tootle's sportsman and late model career.

Lavonia (GA) Speedway Race Director, Brad York provided a number of great photos and information about his dad, the legendary Southern dirt warrior, Bill York.

Also, Dewayne McCannon provided me with page after page of valuable articles and stories from the James "Jabo" Bradberry family collection.

My long time friend and fellow H.E. Vineyard pit crew member, David "Peanut" Jenkins also provided an interesting photo or two.

There were a number of great photos and articles that I used in the book and credit was given for those also.

As always my friend and cover designer, Kent Harrelson was able to look into my head and come up with another great cover for this book. Somehow he always seems to see what I am envisioning in a book cover.

There were a number of other people who played an important part in the writing of this book. Those included, race fans, personal friends, engine builders, drivers, car owners, and pit crew members who knew Estes. To all of you I say thank you. I also want to thank anyone else that I may have left out who played a part in this book.

Finally, I want to thank Herbert Tootle Estes for providing me with a number of memories that will last a lifetime. Thanks, Tootle.

INTRODUCTION

Herbert "Tootle" Estes was born on February 2, 1930 in Knoxville, Tennessee. In his short 52 years of life, Estes would forever cement his place in Southern racing history. Race Fans and drivers alike, remember Estes as a fierce competitor who raced about every kind of race car that had four wheels. Tootle began his racing career in what was known, at the time, as Jalopies. Later, he would go on to race, modifieds, super modifieds, and the winged "Skeeters." Also, NASCAR sportsman, and NASCAR Cup cars; and finally, making a name for himself in the dirt late model ranks.

I watched this Southern racing legend compete in more than a hundred races from the mid-1960's until 1982. Sadly, I was in the pits at Volunteer (TN) Speedway on August 20, 1982 when Tootle won what would be his last race. After winning a hard fought late model race over a stellar field of drivers, Estes died on the way to the hospital of a massive heart attack.

Tootle Estes will always hold a special place in my heart, and that is the reason for the writing of this book. I have many fond memories of Tootle, but the one that will always stand out in my mind was a race at Smoky Mountain Speedway in 1967. I was seventeen years old at the time and had just eloped with my new wife, Elaine. We were traveling up Highway 411 (getting the hell away from our parents). As I passed the Smoky Mountain Speedway sign, I told my wife, what better place to spend our honeymoon than watching a dirt late model race. It was Saturday night May 27, 1967. We got there just before the feature race. There were a great field of cars and drivers that night including, Jim Hunter, Joe Ed Nubert,

L.D. Ottinger, and of course, Tootle Estes. I will never forget the car he was driving that night. It was a bright yellow (and I mean bright yellow) Ford Fairlane with a red #28 on its side. It also had a bright red woodpecker smoking a cigar beside the number. The car had 427cid painted on the hood. For years I wondered what was with the woodpecker? Later, I found out the race car was owned by a man who ran Woody's Auto Clinic in nearby Knoxville. His name was Woody Bradley. So that explained the woodpecker.

A short time later the cars came down the front stretch to take the green flag on the big half-mile dirt oval. Estes started on the inside pole and immediately started pulling away from the field. As the laps were winding down Tootle, driving the car in a power slide all the way around the track, had a half track lead on eventual runner up, Jim Hunter. The car passed us lap after lap with a rooster tail of dust behind that yellow #28. What a way to spend our honeymoon, watching Estes run away from the field.

This book tells the life and times of Herbert "Tootle" Estes. First, taking a brief look at his early life growing up in the late 1930's, including how he got the nickname, "Tootle." We then focus on his early racing career in jalopies, modifieds, super modifieds, and skeeters. Next we examine the NASCAR years in the Sportsman, Convertible, and Cup ranks. Finally, the interest shifts to his late model days and his last win at Volunteer (TN) Speedway on that tragic Saturday night in 1982.

Herbert "Tootle" Estes is a true Southern racing legend and is still talked about over 34 years after he won his last race. He truly was, "The little engine that could."

CHAPTER ONE

HERBERT "TOOTLE" ESTES A LOOK AT HIS EARLY LIFE

Herbert "Tootle" Estes was born during our country's "Great Depression" on February 2, 1930 in the East Tennessee city of Knoxville, Tennessee. Some have said, it was his grandmother, Mamie, who gave Herbert the nickname "Tootle." Others have insisted it was his mother, Beatrice, either way the nickname stuck. The name came from a Simon and Schuster 1940's "Little Golden Book Series for Kids." The book was called, "TOOTLE: THE LITTLE ENGINE THAT COULD, written by Gertrude Crampton. It tells the story of a little train engine named "Tootle" who was the subject of several adventures during the book series. Somehow Tootle's mother or grandmother must have foreseen his future; because in one of the stories about the little train engine one of the lines read, "Green flag means go," and go Tootle Estes did. Beginning in the 1950's, until his death in 1982, Estes won races in about every kind of race car that had four wheels.

Herbert Estes was a member of a large North Knoxville Southern family that included four brothers and two sisters. His brothers were, Paul Jr., Gene, V.A., and Bud. His sisters were, Faye, and Martha. I owe Martha a lot of credit for helping me with Tootle's early life.

By and large, Tootle's father, Paul Sr., was an auto mechanic for most of his life, until health issues took their toll. This is where young Estes probably developed his interest in cars. His mother, Beatrice, took care of the family and home. Later, according to Martha, after the children were older she decided to go to work to help with the family expenses. She worked at a number of jobs in the retail sector, including as a cashier at a couple of super markets in the area, among those were Sharp's Food Market.

Tootle Estes and his wife, Ina Ruth, had two sons, Johnny Lynn, and Rocky. It was Rocky who would follow in his father's footsteps, becoming a pretty good dirt late model driver in his own right. Rocky recently told me, "Probably my biggest thrill in racing was to go head to head with my dad in a dirt late model race. Dad said I am going to race you hard son, if you beat me you are going to have to earn it. Well, I did go on to win that night, and it was one of the hardest wins of my career." The Estes family racing tradition continued with Rocky's son, Rocky Jr., who went on to race at a number of dirt tracks in the East Tennessee area.

Tootle's sister Martha told me recently, "When Tootle was growing up, he liked the things most boys enjoyed doing such as, hunting, golfing, and fishing." She said he loved to fish on nearby Norris Lake. She said, "Tootle always saw the funny side to about everything in life." She went on to tell me a funny fishing story that happened on a trip to Norris Lake. Martha said, "My husband, Tom, and Tootle were fishing one day and all of the sudden my husband hooked a fish, and he kept saying this is going to be a 'beauty', as my husband got the fish closer and closer to the boat, he realized it wasn't as big as he first thought." Old Tootle, true to form said, "It's not going to be a 'beauty' but it is 'cute' little thing Tom."

Later, both Martha and Tootle's son, Rocky, told me a little known fact about Estes. Both said, "Tootle was an avid reader most of his life, and one of his favorite things to read was THE

This is a photo of the Estes Family. That is Martha to the left of Beatrice, the mother. Tootle is behind Martha (Photo provided by Martha Estes Bodie).

READER'S DIGEST." They said he could hardly wait for the new issue to come out each month. When it arrived through the mail they said, "He would read it from cover to cover." Some family members have also told me that Estes loved to read the Bible.

Another longtime friend of Estes, was Tommy Hickman of Soddy-Daisy, Tennessee. Tootle raced a car for Tommy's father, Paul, who owned Paul's Auto Parts. Tommy told me in a recent visit to the auto parts business, "Tootle was good at about everything he set his mind to do, racing, golfing, playing pool, poker, you name it, if he did it he was good at it. He was just a natural at about everything he set his mind to do. He was really good at golf. Tootle had some golf trophies that he kept at home. I think he was more proud of those than his racing trophies."

At about the age of sixteen young Estes took a trip to the old Broadway Speedway in Knoxville to watch the very popular Midget races. Tootle noticed that the drivers would always pull the side brake while going into the turn to slow the cars down. Estes said on the way home that night, "I hope I get the chance to drive one of those Midgets. I won't slow down in the turns."

Just a short while later, Tootle Estes got his first chance at becoming a race car driver, when he drove one of those midgets. Estes knew from the start he had found his passion in life—auto racing. It was a passion he would enjoy for the rest of his life. It was a tribute to his dedication and love of racing, that he would win a dirt late model race on the last night of his life.

Now let's take a look at the racing career of Herbert "Tootle" Estes. It's a journey that would take him, according to some, to over 1200 feature wins, and a place in the National Dirt Late Model Hall of Fame (2009).

CHAPTER TWO

BEING AT THE RIGHT PLACE AT THE RIGHT TIME

In order to understand the evolutionary path that Tootle Estes' racing career traveled, we must first look at the path dirt racing was taking at the time this young Knoxville charger burst onto the racing scene.

Dirt racing's beginnings in the South can probably be traced back to around 1917 at the Atlanta Fairgrounds one-mile dirt oval known as Lakewood Speedway. The first ever race at the track was a match race between two big time rivals, at the time, Barney Oldfield an Ralph DePalma, witnessed by a crowd of over 15,000 race fans.

During the 1920's and into the mid-40's most dirt races in the country were between race cars known as "Big Cars." These race cars were early versions of "open-wheel" sprint cars. The "Big Cars" continued to evolve throughout the period, becoming faster and more sophisticated with each passing year.

Then, in the 1940's Southern race fans and drivers were introduced to a new type of race car. Midget racing had long been very popular among Northern race fans and drivers. The major draw back to midget racing in the North was the short racing season due to the early onslaught of cold weather. It was this cold weather that brought the midget race teams South of the Mason-Dixon line. Southern race fans soon found

A view from the air of the historic Lakewood Speedway. This was a one-mile dirt oval located just South of Atlanta, Ga. (Photo provided by Leon Sells).

a new form of racing to compete with the "Big Cars" that had been popular for several decades.

Also, one must keep in mind that the first half of the 20th Century saw auto racing taking place mainly on state or local fairgrounds at their horse racing facilities. These tracks were usually either a half-mile or longer in length. Most tracks of this type were basically an accident waiting to happen; as the wooden fences, fence posts, and the blinding dust created by the cars were dangerous to both, spectators and drivers alike (for example, the above mentioned Lakewood Speedway had a blinding dust problem for almost its entire existence with several racing deaths the result).

Beginning in the late 1940's and into the 1950's, the winds of change started to take place in the world of auto racing. These changes were twofold in nature. First, racing on fairground horse tracks began to decline because of the above mentioned dangers to both the race fans and drivers.

As a result, from the late 1940's through the early 1960's saw an increase in the number of purpose-built race tracks (tracks built specifically for auto racing). This can clearly be seen in the South where hundreds of tracks sprang up. Among them were; the Peach Bowl (1949) in Atlanta, Georgia; Broadway Speedway (1949) in Knoxville, Tennessee; Boyd's Speedway (1952) in Chattanooga, Tennessee; Golden Strip Speedway (1954) in Fountain Inn, South Carolina; Toccoa Speedway (1955) in Toccoa, Georgia; Banks County Speedway (1955) near Homer, Georgia; Ashway Speedway (1957) in Strawberry Plains, Tennessee; Athens Speedway (1958) in Athens, Georgia; and Cherokee Motor Speedway (also known as Sutalee) (1959) in Canton, Georgia.

Finally, there was the Anderson (SC) Speedway built in the early 1960's. At the time this was one of the premier dirt

This was a typical race car known as a "Big Car" (A pinerest.com photo).

An early midget race car (photo provided by Bob Markos).

tracks in the South. Built by three men (Charlie Mize, Richard Wood, and Rupert Porter) who used the money from the dirt moved from the speedway site to help build I-85, thus helping them finance their track. As you will see this track played a major role in Tootle Estes' racing career.

The second wind of change in racing was the rise of race cars known as "Stock Cars" and their early cousins, the "Jalopy." These early versions of stock cars and/or the Jalopy were fender-less 1930's and 1940's era street cars, usually coupes or sedans. These cars raced somewhat sporadically in the 1930's and 1940's on a number of track's racing programs; before becoming popular toward the end of the 1940's and into the 1950's. In the mid-50's they became known as "Modifieds," because of the liberal modifications made to both the engines and chassis.

Also, beginning around 1955, another group of race cars known as "Sportsman" gained widespread popularity. These were mid-50's Fords and Chevys. They became very popular at most of the Southern dirt tracks. Seemingly overnight, about every dirt track in the South had what became known

This is a 1952 view from the air of Boyd's Speedway. This was one of many "purpose built" tracks that sprang up during the early 1950's (Photo provided by Katy Boyd-Coulter).

as a "Sportsman Class" to go along with the Modifieds. The Sportsman class became the premiere racing class for most Southern dirt tracks going into the 1960's. Many have said the reason for rapid rise of the Sportsman race car, especially in the South was, "There were plenty of junk yards to provide the cars, and plenty of 'good ole boy drivers' to race them." It was sometime during the mid-60's that the Sportsman race cars became known as "Late Models."

As the old saying goes, it appears Tootle Estes was a race driver who was "At the right place at the right time." He was there for the rapid rise of the purpose-built race tracks. But most importantly, he was a driver who had the natural ability to drive the many different types of race cars that were being introduced at the time.

New Speedway Here Eyes Mid-April Opening

By JOHNNY MARTIN
Independent Sports Editor

Despite the recent bad weather, construction is still going ahead at a fast clip on the new Anderson Speedway on Highway 81 (Old Greenville Road) and track officials are busy lining up some of the top drivers in three states to compete here when the oval opens in mid-April.

CONSTRUCTION was slowed during the rain and snow in the area during the past week. But Promoter Charlie Mize points out that the work on the bleachers, which will seat several thousand fans, is near completion.

"If good spring-like weather prevails for about 30 days, we'll be ready for the racing season by about mid-April," Mize said yesterday.

The ⅜th's of a mile clay-oval has high-banked turns and the promoter said that he expects the Anderson Speedway to "be one of the fastest in this section."

The track will feature modified and amateur stock car racing.

THE NEW SIGN pointing the way to the Anderson Speedway, now under construction, goes up in the Piercetown Community. At right of sign is Speedway announcer Matt Phillips and Promoter Charlie Mize while at left is Frank Vickery, track official. (Independent Sports Photo by Jack Hurley).

SOME of the top names in sportsman racing are expected to return to Anderson for the first time since the days of East Park Speedway here.

Tootle Estes of Knoxville, Tenn., Bud Lunsford, Gainesville, Ga., Allen Williamson, Athens, Ga., Buck Simmons, Cornelia, Ga., Mike Adams, Seneca, Charles Smith, Anderson, T. C. Hunt, Atlanta, and Chester Barron, Cornelia, were some of the names of drivers the promoter mentioned as future drivers to appear here.

"Most of these drivers competed here at the old East Park Speedway at one time or another," Mize said. "Some of them are supposed to be building new cars and they'll be racing them here at our weekly Friday night races," he added.

Entrance to the Anderson (SC) Speedway. At the time this was one of the premiere dirt tracks in the South (A Johnny Martin article. Photo by Jack Hurley).

Tootle Estes standing by his #6 jalopy race car shortly after a race (Photo provided by Rocky Estes).

CHAPTER THREE

A RACING CAREER BEGINS

It was the start of the 1953 racing season when a young Knoxville, Tennessee native by the name of Herbert "Tootle" Estes decided to take in the night's racing action at the Broadway Speedway. It was a time when the midget racers were very popular in the South. As Estes watched the racing action, he noticed that the midget drivers were pulling the side hand brake going into the turns to slow the cars down. As mentioned in an earlier chapter, his sister Martha told me Tootle said, "If I ever get a chance to drive one of those I won't use that hand brake." A short while later, Estes got his chance to pilot one of those Midgets. Martha said with a laugh, "Old Tootle used that hand brake too." He told me after the race, "Man those things are going a lot faster than it looks watching them." And so begins the long and exciting racing career of one of the South's best known dirt warriors, Tootle Estes.

It was the early 1950's, and the "Jalopy" race cars (fenderless '30's and '40's sedans and coupes) were at the height of racing popularity. According to some, one of the first cars Estes drove was a Paul "The Ghost" Gose "flat head" Jalopy. A Morristown, Tennessee native, Gose had very good race cars at the time and Tootle was all to happy to be driving for this future racing legend. It didn't take Estes long before he was a frequent visitor to victory lane in the jalopy ranks throughout the East Tennessee area.

Some of his first victories were at Broadway Speedway, Knoxville Raceway; and the Ashway Speedway, where he won

At the time, jalopies were the popular race cars at one of the first races at the Ashway (TN) Speedway. That's Tootle Estes on the pole in the #6 (Photo provided by Wayne Wells).

the first ever race at that track in 1957 over a stellar field of cars that included, H.E. Vineyard, Bill McMahan, Herman Goddard, and the racing Corums out of Maynardville, Tennessee.

As always seems the case in auto racing, "The need for speed" ushered in changes in the Jalopies. These race cars changed dramatically from the late '50's and into the 1960's. Among the changes were, lowering and modifying the race chassis; and using more powerful engines like the GMC 6-cylinders and even some Chevy V-8's to replace the older flat heads. All this to increase speed and handling of what now became known as the "Modified" race car.

It was a "new kid on the block" that was the answer to the rising costs of maintaining and racing a Modified. This "new kid" was the "Sportsman" race car. All over the South, and other parts of the country, Sportsman cars caught on quickly. This was due to their stock appearing look, using mainly 1955-56 Fords and Chevy's. These were perhaps some of the first totally "home built" race cars. These race cars gained popularity from the mid-1950's and continued to be popular well into the '70's when they became known as "Late Models."

Many drivers started driving both the Sportsman and Modified race cars during the racing season. Most tracks had at least two or three racing classes on race night. They included, the Jalopies, Sportsman, and the new Modified class.

Tootle Estes was one of those drivers who chose to drive both the Sportsman and the Modifieds. For the most part, Estes was a full-time driver for his entire racing career. He always said, "I have to race as much as I can in order to put food on the family table."

During the mid-1950's, Estes' main focus was in the in the Sportsman ranks, with some occasional Modified races thrown in when possible. 1956 proved to be his best year in the Sportsman division, taking an amazing 64 checkered flags that year. In addition to Paul Gose's Sportsman cars, Tootle also drove early on for Anderson, South Carolina's James Bradshaw in a number of Modified races. Estes once said in an interview that he and Bradshaw split the winnings 50-50. Tootle's race schedule started on Thursday night and usually ended late on Sunday night, racing sometimes 4 races a week.

This is a photo of an early sportsman Pontiac race car at Smoky Mountain Speedway (Photo provided by Robbie Henry).

If there was a special race on Monday or Tuesday, you could bet Estes would show up for those also, making it as many as 5 races in some weeks.

Tootle quickly progressed from being a local Knoxville area driving ace to becoming a regional threat to win at tracks all over the Southeastern region, in either the Sportsman or the Modified divisions. For example, during the last part of the '50's and into the early '60's, Estes was a frequent winner at tracks like, the Kingsport (TN) Speedway, Mobile (ALA) Speedway; the Athens Speedway in Athens, Georgia; and the Greenwood Fairgrounds Speedway in Greenwood, South Carolina where he scored two wins in one night in August of 1956. As we will see later in this book; Tootle would continue to drive the Sportsman cars, which later became known as Late Models, off and on for the rest of his career.

However, as the 1960's approached, Estes was about to become a force to be reckoned with in the world of Modified racing.

Tootle Estes stands beside his Ace Lawson "modified" #6 race car (Photo provided by Rocky Estes).

Gary L. Parker

CHAPTER FOUR

THE ERA OF THE MODIFIEDS AND SUPER MODIFIED SKEETERS

The dawn of the 1960's saw the popularity of dirt racing continue to gain momentum, especially in the Southeast. Tracks continued to be built, race cars continued to get faster, and the race fans turned out in record numbers.

The Sportsman cars remained a popular fixture at most dirt tracks. However, Modified racing began to move to the forefront again, as drivers and race teams started to modify their race cars and engines in earnest to gain the advantage over the competition. The popularity of the Modified race car was evident all over the country. They were especially well received in the Southeast where a number of drivers would go

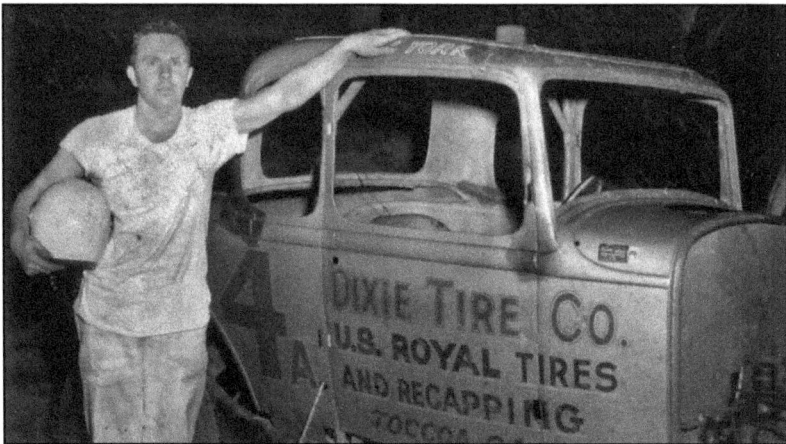

Georgia racing great Bill York was one of Tootle Estes' major competitors in the jalopy, modified, and skeeter ranks in Georgia (Photo provided by Brad York).

Tootle Estes roars by in his James "Jabo" Bradberry Skeeter (Photo provided by Bob Markos).

Side-by-side racing action. That's Estes on the inside in the #6 Skeeter (Photo provided by Bob Markos).

on to etch their place in racing history driving the Modified and Super Modified race cars. Among those pioneer Modified dirt warriors were, Bill York, T.C Hunt, Harold and Freddie Fryar, Charlie Burkhalter, Herman Wise, Charlie Padgett, Cabbage Pendley, Wayne McGuire, Doug Kenimer, Leon Sells, and Charlie Mincey to name but a few of the South's best Modified speed merchants.

However, three other drivers had perhaps the most profound impact on Modified racing in South. They were, a Baldwin, Georgia teenager at the time, known to the dirt racing world as Buck Simmons; the great race driver, engine builder, and chassis guru, Gainesville, Georgia's Bud Lunsford; and finally the focus of this book, Knoxville, Tennessee's driving ace; and a terror on the Modified dirt tracks of the South, Tootle Estes. Estes has the distinction of being probably the only driver ever "barred" from racing in Georgia.

Modified racing once again became the premier division of dirt racing in the late '50's and into the early '60's. The answer to this popularity can be summed up in one word, "speed." Tracks like, Athens Speedway, Toccoa Speedway, Banks County Speedway, and the Greenwood (SC) Fairgrounds Speedway played host to a number of memorable Modified races.

Tootle Estes, Bud Lunsford, Charlie Padgett, Bill York, and others would dominate the early Modified ranks in Georgia and South Carolina. For example, Bud Lunsford had a seven race win streak at the Athens Speedway in a Modified. However, engine builders and chassis builders like, Bud Lunsford, James "Jabo" Bradberry, Ace Lawson, Jim Bradshaw, C.P. Shaw, and others kept finding new ways to gain more speed and better handling from the Modifieds. New innovations like, precision machine work on the engines; the lowering of the chassis and engines was about to reach their limits, especially the carburetor driven, gasoline V-8 engines.

So, around the end of 1962 there would be a new type of Modified introduced to the racing world, "The Super Modified Skeeters." These little winged race cars became an instant hit with both drivers and race fans alike. The reasons were two-fold in nature, "speed and handling."

The name "Skeeter" sounds like a pesky insect known to folks in the South as a mosquito. If we look at both words, we do find a lot in common. For example, a mosquito is a pesky tiny insect with wings, found in swamps or near standing water, and it drinks blood for fuel. Whereas, a skeeter is a pesky small car with a wing on top, bred in Southern race shops; and it drinks alcohol for fuel. But all this aside, the trademark winged Super Modified Skeeters that raced on dirt tracks throughout the South were, nothing more than lightweight (starters and batteries usually removed to save weight), direct drive, fuel-injected, alcohol burning, small block Chevy powered rockets.

According to the late Herman Collins, owner of Knoxville, Tennessee's legendary West Haven Auto Parts, "Tootle won around 1200 races during his career. I'd say over 800 of them were in modifieds and skeeters."

Knoxville, Tennessee's Tootle Estes began his reign of Modified racing terror in Georgia and South Carolina in the late 1950's. Two of the first Modified teams Estes raced for was Cleveland, Tennessee's, Ace Lawson; and Anderson, South Carolina's, Jim Bradshaw. Almost from the start, Tootle became the man to beat at tracks like, the Athens Speedway, Toccoa Speedway and Banks County Speedway. He became a frequent winner over many of the stars of the modified ranks at the time including, Bud Lunsford, Charlie Mincey, Bill York, Charlie Burkhalter, Charlie Padgett, Buck Simmons, and a number of other regional dirt warriors.

It was during the early '60's that Tootle would become a dominate force in the modified ranks. Estes came to the Greenville (SC) Fairgrounds Speedway in Ace Lawson's 1934 modified sedan and won, he scored another checkered flag the next night at Anderson (SC) Speedway. At Toccoa (GA) Speedway he made it three in a row the very next night. This winning streak would continue for 16 straight races until he wrecked the car while leading in another race. Lawson made repairs to the car at his shop and Estes started winning again the very next weekend.

In the mid-1960's, Tootle would team up with "The king of the super modifieds," the Athens, Georgia car builder, James "Jabo" Bradberry. Together Estes and Bradberry would dominate the super modified ranks in the South for several years. Again, because of the trademark wing on top, and the fuel injected engines these ultra fast little race cars became known as "Skeeters." As I mentioned earlier, Estes won a record 29 straight races during one span. This resulted in him being banned from racing for a while in the state of Georgia. This was something that has been a rarity in the sport of auto racing.

According to Tootle's son, Rocky, his dad's best year in the modified ranks was in 1964 when he scored 49 feature wins in Georgia, South Carolina, and East Tennessee. According to some, in one period of racing modifieds, Estes was thought to have won 84 of the 104 races he entered.

As you will see from the many racing articles, taken from newspapers and racing magazines at the end of this chapter, only a few drivers were able to mount any type of win streaks during the Estes "Period of Domination." Two of those drivers were, Gainsville's Bud Lunsford and the teenage racing phenomenon from Baldwin, Georgia, Buck Simmons.

A special thanks is in order at this time to Dewayne Mc-Cannon for providing these valuable articles from the James "Jabo" Bradberry family collection. They span the years from the early 1960's until the early part of 1966.

Lunsford Wins Heat, Main Event At Track

Gainesville's Bud Lunsford added two more stars to his racing crown this weekend at the Athens Speedway, winning the second heat in the modified event and also crossing the finish line ahead of everyone else in the main event.

Lunsford, the driver with the most wins in last year's competition at the Speedway, copped the two wins from arch-rivals Tootle Estes and T. C. Hunt. Lunsford flashed to victory a total of 11 times in the 1960 season.

Almost every race at the Speedway has been decided by these three drivers this year. Always strong contenders, they are among the best at the track.

The slam-bang jalopy event, which opens up the activity each week, was won by James Green from Logansville. Johnny Coffee, an Athens boy, crashed in second.

The huge amateur event, sporting a 19 car field, was racked up by Athens' own Charlie Burkhalter. Another Athenian, Lewis Cooper, made it a clean sweep for the Classic City in the Am event.

The 19 entries made the race one of the largest amateur events ever assembled at the Athens Speedway, according to a track spokesman.

A driver from neighboring South Carolina copped the first heat race in the modified events. Doris "Sosebee of Anderson, S.C., took the heat laurels.

Lundsford won the second heat, and the consolation event was taken by Cummings' Cabbage Pendley.

Lunsford rolled to victory in the main event, also. Backing him up were Estes. who races out of Knoxville, Tenn., and Atlanta's Hunt, an old hand at the Athens track. who took third place.

The races are held every Saturday night. Warm-ups begin at 7:30, and the first race gets underway at 8 p.m. Admission is $2 per person, with children under 12 admitted free when accompanied by adults.

Athens Draws New Drivers

ATHENS — Art Mitchell, who finished second in the race at Jacksonville a week ago, will be one of the newcomers at the Athens Speedway races here Sunday afternoon. He is a definite challenge to Harold Fryer, Bud Lunsford and Tootle Estes, the kingbees of racing in this section.

Promoter Bill Cooley has invited 50 drivers and car owners to be here for the Sunday races, indicating a record number of entries may be on hand.

Five races will be held Sunday, the first starting at 2:30 o'clock. They will include two heats, consolation, the amateur main and the 50-lap modified feature.

The weather promises to be favorable to racing.

Saturday Night Speedway Races To Be Inverted

The agenda for Saturday night's racing at the Athens Speedway will be all mixed up. The race will be run in "inverted order," with last week's winnes starting in the rear.

A full slate of racing was run Tuesday night, with the feature being the annual 100-lap midseason championship.

Action got underway with the 20 lap amateur event, with Athens' own Charlie Burkhalter walking off with the victory. Tommy Alewine and Lewis Cooper, both of Athens, took second and third place respectively, over the 20 car field.

The jalopy race, with a 15 car field, was next on the program, and Johnny Coffee, Athens, copped the first place prize. Billy Whitehead and Elbert Smith finished behind him.

In the feature race, the 100-lapper Freddie Frayar took all the marbles. The Chattanooga lad crossed the finish line in front of second-place Herman Wise of Lavonia third-place T. C. Hunt, Atlanta, and, in fourth-position, Chattanooga's Harold Fryar.

Bud Lunsford Eyes Eighth Speedway Win

Bud Lunsford of Gainesville, winner of the 40-lap feature race at the Athens Speedway for the past seven weeks will be eyeing his eighth straight win in Saturday night's race.

Lunsford will be defending his position against other top drivers such as T. C. Hunt of Atlanta, Howard Corbin of Chamblee, J. C. Hendrix of Griffin, Tootle Estes of Knoxville, Tenn., and Eddie MacDonald of Phenix City, Ala.

T. C. Hunt, who was pushing Lunsford for first place in last week's race before the race was called because of a track rule, may not be able to make this week's races.

Tootle Estes and J. C. Hendrix who finished in the top six last week will be pushing Lunsford for the purse this week.

President of the Speedway, Bill Cooley, has announced that a bonus will be given to any driver that beats Lunsford in the feature event in addition to the regular prize money, but only if Lunsford finishes the race.

Other events on Saturday night's card are two heat races, a consolation race, amateur race, and a 10-lap jalopy race.

The warm-ups are scheduled to begin at 8:15 and the first race gets underway at 8:30.

Last week the speedway had one of the largest fields yet and President Cooley expects even more drivers for this week's ce.

Gary L. Parker

Lunsford Cops Victory at Hall Speedway, Then Sells Racer That Has Taken 21 Wins

Bud Lunsford's feature victory at the Hall County Speedway here Friday night will be his last win in the speedy, custom-built car that has helped him to become the leading stock car driver in this area.

Lunsford sold his auto to T. C. Hunt, Atlanta driver, Saturday morning and plans to "lay off" racing for awhile or drive a car owned by someone else.

The young Gainesvillian had driven the car to 21 feature race victories this season.

Friday night, Lunsford finished in front of Tootle Estes, Claude Mauldin and Charlie Burkhalter in the 50-lap feature. But also took the second heat and tied with Estes in the fast-car dash.

Estes was driving a new car with a 1957 Corvette motor, but was still unable to best Lunsford.

Robert Weatherford of Gainesville took first in the consolation race as Burkhalter copped the first heat.

Only 10 cars showed up for the event.

BURKHALTER SPINS THROUGH TURN

... Athens Driver Took Heat Victory

Bud Lunsford Cops Victory

TOCCOA — Bud Lunsford won the main event at the Toccoa Speedway Saturday night as the stock car racing season opened here. T. C. Hunt, Howard Corbin and Charlie Burkhalter finished in that order behind him.

Lunsford and Hunt were heat winners.

Carl Stonecipher was first in the amateur main, trailed closely by Bobby Derrick and Fireball Roberts.

York Winner Banks Race

CORNELIA — Bill York of Toccoa won the main event of the modified-sportsman stock car race here tonight, finishing second ahead of both Carl Stonecipher and the rain. The clouds opened just as the checkered flag went down. Curly Halford was third and Chester Barron fourth.

Wayne Garrison and York won the heats, Dick Hunnicutt the consolation and Halford a special trophy dash.

Buck Simmons Wins 2 Races

Buck Simmons of Athens, Ga., won two 50-lap modified races at Kingsport Speedway Saturday night as the track held its annual Labor Day weekend events.

Simmons was ahead at the end of the first 50 laps. The field was then reversed, putting the front cars to the back, but he leadfooted his way back into the lead.

Winner of the 40-lap amateur race was Fred Clevenger of Kingsport.

RACING ROUNDUP

WESTMINSTER SPEEDWAY — Saturday night's winners: Amateur heats — Sam Kelly and Sam Dickson. Sportsman heats — Marvin Moore and Tommy Roberts. Jalopy events L. J. Honea, Dawson Alexander, and Sam Owens. Amateur main — 1. Sam Dickson, 2 — Floyd Holcomb, 3 — Benny Evatt. Sportsman main — 1 — Buck Simmons, 2 — Marvin Moore, 3. — Floyd Holcomb.

STOCK CAR RACES

TONITE 7:30 P. M.
7 BIG EVENTS
3 MAIN EVENTS
4 HEAT RACES
Over 100 Laps Racing.
A $25 Bonus To 1st Place Sportsman Driver Who Outruns Buck Simmons Legally.
Come And See If This Can Be Done.

WESTMINSTER SPEEDWAY

Located on Coffee Road Off Highway 76
WESTMINSTER, S. C.

31

Sudderth's Peach Win Big Blow to Lunsford

Johnny Sudderth is a man who never lets an opportunity slip away from him. He proved that Sunday night at the Peach Bowl.

Running behind Bud Lunsford for the first 33 laps of the 40-lap feature Sudderth found an opening on the outside when another driver blew a tire up front, gave his skeeter the gas and swept by Lunsford.

He held the lead the rest of the way. This was the third show of the year at the Peach Bowl and once again a new winner emerged. Lunsford and Tod-

dle Estes were past winners.

Sudderth also won the first semi and Lunsford won the second semi.

A crowd estimated at 2,000 was on hand.

1st Heat—Bud Lunsford, Donald Fowler, Charlie Padgett; 2nd Heat—Johnny Sudderth, Toddle Estes, J. C. Hendrix; 3rd Heat—C. A. Pendley, Howard Corbin, O. H. Jones; 1st Semi—Johnny Sudderth, Toddle Estes, J. C. Hendrix; 2nd Semi—Bud Lunsford, T. C. Hunt, Katron Soseebee; Feature—Johnny Sudderth, Bud Lunsford, Toddle Estes.

Estes Captures Second Peach Bowl Feature

Herb "Tootle" Estes of Athens blazed across the finish line first to win the 40-lap feature race at the Peach Bowl Speedway Sunday night. This was his second win in four tries at the Peach Bowl.

Estes took the lead away from Bill Hamby of Smyrna on the 15th lap and led the rest of the way.

Johnny Sudderth of Atlanta was way out front of the pack until the 13th lap when his battery went dead and he had to pull out of the race. Hamby took the lead for two laps and then discovered he had not regassed for the feature and had to pull out.

Bud Lunsford of Gainesville finished second and Cabbage Pendley of Cumming took the third spot.

Sudderth won the 10-lap preliminary and 12-lap semifeature with ease.

In the second 12-lap semifea-

ture, T. C. Hunt of Atlanta and Bud Lunsford ran one of the closest events of the night. Lunsford breathed down Hunt's neck all 12 laps but Hunt won by a half car link.—WYNN.

10-lap preliminary — Howard Corbin (Chamblee), Charlie Padgett (Marietta). Don Fowler, (Atlanta). 10-lap preliminary—Johnny Sudderth (Atlanta), Bill Hemby (Smyrna), J. C. Hendrix (Griffin). 10-lap preliminary—Eddie McDonald (Columbus), Cabbage Pendley (Cumming), Mike Price (Atlanta). 12-lap semi-feature — Johnny Sudderth, Bill Hemby, Charlie Padgett. 12-lap semi-feature—T. C. Hunt (Atlanta), Bud Lunsford (Gainesville), Mike Price. 40-lap feature—Toodle Estes (Athens), Bud Lunsford, Cabbage Pendley, Charlie Padgett, T. C. Hunt.

Bud Lunsford Athens Winner

ATHENS —Bud Lunsford of Garnesville won the feature event at Athens Speedway Saturday night, with Tootle Estes coming in second in the 14-car field.

James Beauchamp and Grier Dawson, both of Athens ran one-two in the amateur race in which 14 cars started.

Bobby Acker won the jalopy race followed by Junior Fouche.

Lunsford Is Winner Of 2

CORNELIA — A racing program that ran into midnight saw Bud Lunsford of Gainesville, capture both 35-lap features at Banks County Speedway near here Saturday night.

Lunsford, runing fourth through the 29th lap of the first race, shot into the lead and to victory when the three lead cars wrecked. Jerry Smith of Chattanooga, Charlie Padgett of Marietta and Charlie Burkhalter of Athens finished behind Lunsford in that order.

Tootle Estes of Knoxville led the second 35-lap feature for 34 laps, but as he and Lunsford, running almost side-by-side, passed a slower car going into the 35th lap. Estes hit the retaining wall and blew a tire. Lunsford won easily. T. C. Hunt of Atlanta was second, Bill Parnell, also of Atlanta, finished third, and Robert Weatherford of Gainesville was fourth.

Bill York of Toccoa won the first heat, Hunt the second, and Eddie Grant captured the amateur, Windell Roach second.

Lavonia Man Dash Winner

ELBERTON — Herman Wise, who was racing in the amateur division a year ago, had his best day as a pro here Sunday when he won the trophy dash and second heat at Twin Lakes Raceway.

Wise kept up the pace in the 50-lap feature but finished second to Tootle Estes of Knoxville. Sam Smith of Union was third and Claude Donavon of Knoxville was fourth.

Donavon won the first heat.

York Crashes But Wins Race

CORNELIA—Bill York crashed through the fence in the second heat but was not injured, nor was his car extensively damaged, and he came back to win the modified sportsman main event at Banks County Speedway Saturday night.

Marvin Moore and Bob Derrick were heat winners, while George Randlett and Carl Stonecipher roared to a dead heat finish to share honors in the consolation which was stopped in the first lap when Curley Hallford flipped.

Amos Simmons won the jalopy race.

32

Lunsford On Victory Trail Again

Bud Lunsford of Gainesville, who started the 1960 season blazing the victory trail and carrying the longest winning streak at the Athens Speedway, is at it again, by winning the 40-lap feature race Saturday night.

Lunsford finished first in the thrill-packed 40-lap Feature race Saturday night. Herb "Toodle" Estes of Knoxville, Tenn. ran a close second until he was forced out by mechanical trouble. J. C. Hendrix of Griffin was second, Herman Wise of Lavonia, third, and Estes, fourth.

In the Consolation race Saturday night, Herman Wise, who took third in the Feature race, finished first.

C. A. Hardy of Nicholson won the Amateur race and Clarence Smith of Athens ran a close second.

In the 10-lap Jalopy race James Green of Logansville finished first and Jerry Shedd of Winder was second.

A large field of over 50 cars was present for Saturday night's races but Speedway President Bill Cooley says he expects more cars for the 30-lap Jalopy Championship race planed for next Saturday night.

President Cooley added that a change has been made, and that races are now getting underway at 8:00.

Herb Estes Enters Labor Day Classic

Herb "Tootle" Estes of Knoxville, Tenn., one of the top drivers at the Athens Speedway, has entered the list for the Labor Day 100-mile modified race at Atlanta's Lakewood Speedway.

Estes, who won last week's prize in Athens, will be driving his Chevrolet-powered Ford.

Heading the line-up is Bobby Allison of Miami, who is currently in third place in NASCAR national point standings.

Other entries from Knoxville are Jim Hunter with his fuel injection Chevrolet-powered Ford, and Bill McMahan in his Buick.

Chattanooga, Tenn., will be represented by Harold Fryar and Bob Burchman in Chevrolet-powered Fords, and Otis Gaither with his Pontiac.

Roswell, Ga., furnishes Harold Smith, Woody Coleman and J. H. Chester in '57 Chevrolets.

Time trials for the Labor Day Classic at Lakewood begins at 1:30 and the 100-miler is set to

Estes Claims Feature Win At Speedway

An out-of-starter Friday night shattered the lengthy reign of Athenian Charlie Burkhalter and Marietta's Charlie Padgett at the Athens Speedway.

Tootle Estes of Knoxville, Tenn., grabbed the lead at the start and held it all the way to win the featured 50-lap Open competition race. Burkhalter was forced out of the race because of mechanical difficulties. Padgett never got started: he was sidelined by mechanical problems during the pre-race heats.

In the 20-lap Jalopy race Obie Mosely of Lawrenceville roared under the flag in first place ahead of Alfred Graham of Dewey Rose. William Casper of Camden captured third, Charles Stamey of Athens fourth, and Tyre Dodd of Winder fifth.

Victor Casper led at the halfway mark but blew a tire and had to drop out of the race.

Roy Nalley won the 30-lap Amateur, with Gerald Crowe of Winder coming in second, Wild Man Worley of Elberton third, Ed Brown of Hartwell fourth and Dennis Langford of Athen fifth.

Back of Estes in the 50-lap open were Dub Meelor of Athens, Jabez Jones of Lavonia, Cabbage Pendley of Covington, Bobby Young of Due West, S. C., and Walter Noussee of Athens — the only six of the starting 16 to finish the race

Saturday night's program of 120 laps was rained out.

Hunt Wins At Athens

ATHENS — T. C. Hunt, with Charlie Padgett on his bumper all the way, won the 50-lap main event at the Athens Speedway here Friday night. Hunt, who took the lead at the start and held it, could not shake Padgett. Next three finishers in order were Bobby Young, Howard Corbin and Charles Burkhalter.

Hunt and Corbin won the heats, and Bud Lunsford picked up the consolation purse. Wilton Watkins whizzed ahead for top prize in the amateur main.

Estes Avoids Pileup, Wins At Speedway

Tootle Estes of Knoxville, Tenn., avoided near disaster on the first turn, then went on to capture first place in the 40-lap feature race for the second week in a row at the Athens Speedway Saturday night.

At the first turn Ed Luther, in the pole position, whipped the rear of his car into the path of Estes, who was coming up fast preparing to pass on the curve. Instead, Estes ran up and over the right rear tire of Luther's car and lost control of his car as he went spinning into the retaining wall of the second turn.

He regained control as he went sliding down the backstretch, but he left behind him eight cars that had tangled trying to avoid Estes on that turn.

But Saturday it was all Estes. He led from the first lap and was never challenged. Charlie Padgett ran second for the first 17 laps but had to bow out because of mechanical trouble. Charlie Burkhalter finished second, ahead of Athens' Shorty Vinson, Curly Allison of Atlanta, and Lewis Cooper of Athens.

In other events William Casper of Campton swept first in the jalopy, with Athenian Danny Watkins claiming second. James Beechamp of Nicholson continued to dominate the 30-lap amateur race.

Bud Lunsford Wins At Athens

Special To Independent

ATHENS — Bud Lunsford roared across the finish line here Friday night to win top money in the 50-lap main event at the Athens Speedway. Trailing him in order were Charlie Burkhalter, Katron Sosebee and Charles Smith. Lunsford also was a heat winner along with Charlie Padgett. Wilton Watkins won the amateur event. Slick Lewallen was second.

Sudderth's Peach Win Big Blow to Lunsford

Johnny Sudderth is a man who never lets an opportunity slip away from him. He proved that Sunday night at the Peach Bowl.

Running behind Bud Lunsford for the first 33 laps of the 40-lap feature Sudderth found an opening on the outside when another driver blew a tire up front, gave his skeeter the gas and swept by Lunsford.

He held the lead the rest of the way. This was the third show of the year at the Peach Bowl and once again a new winner emerged. Lunsford and Toddle Estes were past winners.

Sudderth also won the first semi and Lunsford won the second semi.

A crowd estimated at 2,000 was on hand.

1st Heat—Bud Lunsford, Donald Fowler, Charlie Padgett; 2nd Heat—Johnny Sudderth, Toddle Estes, J. C. Hendrix; 3rd Heat—C. A. Pendley, Howard Corbin, O. H. Jones; 1st Semi—Johnny Sudderth, Toddle Estes, J. C. Hendrix; 2nd Semi—Bud Lunsford, T. C. Hunt, Katron Sossebee; Feature—Johnny Sudderth, Bud Lunsford, Toodle Estes.

Estes Captures Second Peach Bowl Feature

Herb "Tootle" Estes of Athens blazed across the finish line first to win the 40-lap feature race at the Peach Bowl Speedway Sunday night. This was his second win in four tries at the Peach Bowl.

Estes took the lead away from Bill Hamby of Smyrna at the turn of the 15th lap and led the rest of the way.

Johnny Sudderth of Atlanta was way out front of the pack until the 13th lap when his battery went dead and he had to pull out of the race. Hamby took the lead for two laps and then discovered he had not regassed for the feature and had to pull out.

Bud Lunsford of Gainesville finished second and Cabbage Pendley of Cumming took the third spot.

Sudderth won the 10-lap preliminary and 12-lap semifeature with ease.

In the second 12-lap semifeature, T. C. Hunt of Atlanta and Bud Lunsford ran one of the closest events of the night. Lunsford breathed down Hunt's neck all 12 laps but Hunt won by a half car link.—WYNN.

10-lap preliminary — Howard Corbin (Chamblee), Charlie Padgett (Marietta), Don Fowler (Atlanta). 10-lap preliminary—Johnny Sudderth (Atlanta), Bill Hemby (Smyrna), J. C. Hendrix (Griffin). 10-lap preliminary—Eddie McDonald (Columbus), Cabbage Pendley (Cumming), Mike Price (Atlanta). 12-lap semi-feature — Johnny Sudderth, Bill Hemby, Charlie Padgett. 12-lap semi-feature—T. C. Hunt (Atlanta), Bud Lunsford (Gainesville), Mike Price. 40-lap feature—Toodle Estes (Athens), Bud Lunsford, Cabbage Pendley, Charlie Padgett, T. C. Hunt.

Bud Lunsford Athens Winner

ATHENS —Bud Lunsford of Garnesvile won the feature event at Athens Speedway Saturday night, with Tootle Estes coming in second in the 14-car field.

James Beauchamp and Grier Dawson, both of Athens ran one-two in the amateur race in which 14 cars started.

Bobby Acker won the jalopy race followed by Junior Fouche.

Lunsford Is Winner Of 2

CORNELIA — A racing program that ran into midnight saw Bud Lunsford, of Gainesville, capture both 35-lap features at Banks County Speedway near here Saturday night.

Lunsford, runing fourth through the 29th lap of the first race, shot into the lead and to victory when the three lead cars wrecked. Jerry Smith of Chattanooga, Charlie Padgett of Marietta and Charlie Burkhalter of Athens finished behind Lunsford in that order.

Tootle Estes of Knoxville led the second 35-lap feature for 34 laps, but as he and Lunsford, running almost side-by-side, passed a slower car going into the 35th lap. Estes hit the retaining wall and blew a tire. Lunsford won easily. T. C. Hunt of Atlanta was second, Bill Parnell, also of Atlanta, finished third, and Robert Weatherford of Gainesville was fourth.

Bill York of Toccoa won the first heat, Hunt the second, and Eddie Grant captured the amateur, Windell Roach second.

Lavonia Man Dash Winner

ELBERTON — Herman Wise, who was racing in the amateur division a year ago, had his best day as a pro here Sunday when he won the trophy dash and second heat at Twin Lakes Raceway.

Wise kept up the pace in the 50-lap feature but finished second to Tootle Estes of Knoxville. Sam Smith of Union was third and Claude Donavon of Knoxville was fourth.

Donavon won the first heat.

York Crashes But Wins Race

CORNELIA—Bill York crashed through the fence in the second heat but was not injured, nor was his car extensively damaged, and he came back to win the modified sportsman main event at Banks County Speedway Saturday night.

Marvin Moore and Bob Derrick were heat winners, while George Randlett and Carl Stonecipher roared to a dead heat finish to share honors in the consolation which was stopped in the first lap when Curley Halliford flipped.

Amos Simmons won the jalopy race.

Gary L. Parker

Final Race Set This Afternoon

The final race of the fall season will be run at the Athens Speedway Sunday afternoon. The program starts at 2:30 p.m.

Tootle Estes, Knoxville, Tenn., who won the opening race and Harold Fryer, Chattanooga, Tenn., winner of last week's main event, ...gured the men to beat in the 50 lap feature event. The man given the best chance of outdriving them is Bud Lunsford, Gainesville, who lost out last week due to mechanical trouble. Estes was also forced out last Sunday when his racer developed trouble. Among the other contenders will be Charlie Burkhalter and Hugh Jones from the Athens area.

Two heats, a consolation race, 30 lap amateur event, and the 50 lap modified main event are on the program at the new Athens Speedway located off the Atlanta highway.

Open Returns To Speedway

Athens Speedway officials Monday announced the return of the "Open Competition" for super-modifieds, sportsman, rails, etc. tonight in a special 50-lap race. Starting time is 8:30.

Bud Lunceford of Gainesville, Tootle Estes of Knoxville, Herman Wise and Howard Corbin of Atlanta, Charlie Padgett (driving the super-modified racer which won the last 50-lap open feature) and Buck Simmons will be the top contenders facing the Sportsman drivers, led by top money winner of the current season, Charlie Mincey of Atlanta.

Three 10-lap heat races are on the program which will include Amateur and Jalopy events as a preliminary to the popular 50-lap feature. Admission for the 130-lap program will be $2.50.

Padgett Wins At Speedway, Nosing Estes

Charlie Padgett of Marietta used a sudden burst of speed in the final few seconds Monday to win the 100-lap championship sportsman race in a special Labor Day event at the Athens Speedway.

Trailing Tootle Estes of Knoxville, Tenn. with about 100 yards left, Padgett ended the see-saw battle which had gone on between himself and Estes throughout the race with a last second surge, winning by a half-car length. Charlie Burkhalter and Dub Meelor, both of Athens, finished third and fourth.

In the jalopy event Marvin Pike of Atlanta finished first, followed by Billy Churchill of Athens and Alfred Graham of Dewey Rose. The event went 20 laps.

Hugh McMichael of Logarville captured the championship in the 30-lap amateur race after moving up from the rear in the first 15-laps. James Beacham , of Nicholson and Jackie Shedd of Winder placed second and third.

Athens Speedway Attracts Crowd

More than 3,000 avid auto racing fans attended the races Friday night at Athens Speedway, seven miles out on the Atlanta Highway. Promoter Bill Cooley said the crowd was among the largest ever attracted to the speedway.

The Amateur race was won by Slick Lewallen, of Cornelia.

The first heat race was won by Bud Lunsford, of Gainesville, with Charlie Burkhalter of Athens second.

The second heat race saw Howard Corbin, Buford, cross the line first with Leon Segars, Carnesville, second.

The feature race and hotly contested with Howard Corbin winning first prize money of $180; Charlie Padgett, Dallas, Ga., driving a car owned by Pete Hancock, Athens, took second and $130, while Charles Smith of Anderson, S. C., was third to win $95, and Leon Smith, Carnesville, fourth.

Estes Wins But No Bonus

Tootle Estes of Knoxville, Tenn., was a new winner at the Athens Speedway Saturday night, but he didn't collect a bonus.

A $50 bonus goes to the new winner in the Sportsman Division each week, but only if the previous week's winner finishes the race.

Charlie Burkhalter, winner a week ago, blew a tire on the 17th lap and was eliminated. Estes led all the way, with the caution light being on only twice in the first 30 laps and only five times during the entire race. It was one of the fastest races on the local track this season.

Charlie Padgett was second to Estes and Willis Langford, Athens, third.

Wild Bill Caspar of Campton won the Jalop event. Pete Bullock won the amater race after a collision took out front runners Freddy Williams and James Beechamp. Jackie Sheed, Winder, was second and Bobby Durden, Loganville, third.

Tennessee Race Driver Provides Local Competition

A ennessean is new competition for the familiar racers at the Athens Speedway and Tootle Estes will be on hand Saturday night for the 120-lap program which was rained out a week ago.

The Knoxville native, a popular modified driver, will be racing for the first time in the Sportsman division after capturing the big 50-lap special modified feature in the last race at the local track.

Drawn to Athens by the $50 bonus for a new winner in the Sportsman feature, Estes will be driving a new Chevrolet-powered sportsman racer built and owned by James Bradberry, Athens.

The 40-lap Sportsman feature event will be part of the racing action that includes Amateur and Jalopy events. The show begins at 8:30 p.m.

Charlie Padgett, midseason sportsman champ and a familiar winner in the sportsman field, will be one of several contenders in sportsman competition along with Estes. Others are Charlie Burkhalter, Reece Lester, Claude Mauldin and Dub Meeler.

35

WORK IS NEARING completion on Anderson Speedway, located 11 miles from Anderson in the Piercetown Community. (Independent Sports Photo by Kayle Turner from Carolina Aero Service Plane piloted by Lee Blume).

Anderson Speedway To Be Ready For April Opening

By JOHNNY MARTIN
Independent Sports Editor

Construction is nearing completion on the new Anderson Speedway, located on Highway 81 (Old Greenville Highway), in Piercetown Community, about 11 miles from the city.

The fast three-eights clay oval is due to be finished by April 1 with the first race 10 to 14 days later.

The Anderson Speedway will have several thousand bleacher-type seats and will feature modern concession stands and rest room facilities.

The speedway, owned by the Anderson S p e e d w a y Corp., Charles Mize, president and treasurer, Richard Wood, vice-president, and Ruper Porter, secretary, will also feature new lighting and public address systems. There will be 12 acres of parking area.

Promoter Charlie Mize says that full-body modifieds will be featured with no restrictions on motor specifications. The racers will be running V-8 overhead valve engines. "The only restriction is that there can be no straight drive transmissions, each car must be able to crank under its own power," Mize explained.

It is planned to have races every Friday night at the Anderson Speedway with race-time at 8:30. Drivers from Georgia, South Carolina, and Tennessee are expected to be regulars.

Amateur racing will also be featured. The engines in the amateur division will be strictly stock. "The grading is completed," pointed out Mize. "The fences, lights, and stands are still under construction."

With the opening of Anderson Speedway, it will mark the return of racing to the City of Hospitality. For many years, East Park Speedway provided local fans with weekly racing but when it terminated several years ago, Anderson fans had to turn elsewhere for racing events.

"We are hoping to bring racing back to Anderson in a big way," concluded Mize. "We've had so many requests to do so. . .and we feel that our track will be one of the best in the area,' he said.

Anderson Speedway

'CHAMPIONS' TAKE AIM AT BUD TONIGHT; RACES START AT 8

Champions from many area race tracks will be in the modified main event at the Anderson Speedway tonight.

Buck Simmons, the 15-year-old driver from Cornelia, Ga. who rose from amateur to full modified in two years was the 1962 champion at Westminster Speedway.

Bill York, 1962 champ at Keowee Speedway, Homer Owens of Duncan, Fountain Inn Speedway champion, and Charlie Burkhalter, 1962 racing champ at Athens Speedway, are three other champions in tonight's main event lineup.

Bud Lunsford of Gainesville, Ga., champ at Toccoa and Banks County Speedways last year, is doing the same at Anderson Speedway this year and will put his unbeaten Anderson record on the line t night against this lineup champions.

Tootle Estes of Knoxvill Tenn. has been a consta threat to Lunsford here all se son. He has finished secor more than any other driver a night for the 8 o'clock, 100-la six-event program.

Charlie Smith, who has ha hard luck with his racer, h been testing his fuel injectc Chevy this past week and is r ported ready for tonight events. Estes has had tw weeks to get his fuel injecto Chevy in top condition.

The purse tonight is over $1 100 with $200 going to the fir place winner in the modifie feature. Amateur racing, wi also be featured tonight at th new Anderson oval located c

TWO GREENWOOD mechanics, Durward Brunson and Fred Simpson put finishing touches on one of two cars scheduled to be in action tonight at Anderson Speedway. Buck Fulp, Anderson, will be driving No. 26 and Harvey Corley, Greenwood, will be piloting No. 3. (Independent Sports photo by Gene Cantrell.)

RACING ROUNDUP

Two new drivers and a more powerful Tootle Estes' racer will take aim on Bud Lunsford's 15-race win streak at Anderson Speedway tonight. James Bradberry, owner of Estes' racer, says that he has installed a stroker engine in the No. 6 machine. Estes has been second to Lunsford 12 times.

The two new drivers expected at the Anderson oval tonight are Buck Fulp, Anderson, and Harvey Corey, Greenwood. Both will pilot new racers. Fulp is known as one of the top drivers in the South in the sports car division. A large field of modified drivers from Georgia, South Carolina, and Tennessee are expected for the 8 o'clock program.

Bud Lunsford Wins Again!

Bud Lunsford paced the pack last night at the Anderson Speedway, finishing ahead of Tootle Estes and Buck Simmons to win the modified feature race. Lunsford and Roamey Medlock were heat winners.

Horace York won the amateur championship race, followed by George Randlett in second. Heats went to York and Dewey Tumblin.

Race Here Friday, 8:30

Anderson Speedway opens it new racing season Friday night with a seven-event program starting at 8:30 p.m.

Promoter Charlie Mize said that the 8:30 starting time had been necessitated because of a revival being held at the Friendship Baptist Church near the race track. All other Friday night racing programs will start at 8 o'clock.

Amateur, sportsman, jalopy, and modified racers will be featured every Friday.

Mize also said that in Friday's opening race Doris Sosebee of Anderson will be driving last year's Tootle Estes' car. Estes will pilot a new car this season.

Anderson Speedway To Be Improved; Opener Nears

With the opening race at Anderson Speedway less than three weeks away, work is underway to make improvements for the convenience of the spectators.

Promoter Charlie Mize said that concrete steps have been poured at the main entrance and also to the concession stand.

Prior to the opening date of April 3 (Friday), the track will be open to drivers for trial runs Saturday afternoon March 28. The public is invited.

Mize stated that with the entry of eight new drivers in the modified division, he expects this to be a good season and that competition will be keen. New faces will include: Bill York, Hugh Jones, T. C. Hunt, Jim Bradshaw, Herman Wise, Jabez Jones, Tommy Roberts, and Lewis Cooper, whose car engine will be equipped with a blower. York will drive a racer powered with a Cobra engine.

New clay will be hauled in to fill the low places that caused a mud hole last year. Mize also said that races will not be run in mud as was the case last year.

The new jalopy division has caused much interest. Aubrey Attaway was the first driver in this division to enter. The amateur division will be allowed an 0.80 overbore for the first time. This, of course, means the cars in this division will be faster.

12   Independent Anderson, S. C., Fri., April 3, 1964

Anderson Speedway Opens New Season Here Tonight

TOOTLE ESTES   **BUCK SIMMONS**

Drivers who had to settle for 2nd and 3rd place finishes last racing season at Anderson Speedway will put new cars on the track tonight in the '64 race opener here in an effort to beat last year's big winner, Bud Lunsford of Gainesville, Ga.

First race is at 8:30.

Bud Lunsford copped 19 main events last season and Tootle Estes ran 2nd most of the time. Buck Simmons 3rd most of the time.

Lunsford will be back tonight in the same car he drove last season while Estes and Simmons will pilot new racing machines.

Estes will drive a 1932 B model Ford coach with a 1964 fuel injector Chevy engine.

Simmons will be driving a Model A Ford Coupe with a 1964 fuel injection Chevy engine.

The 16-year-old Simmons began this racing career at 14, in the amateur division He was track champ at Westminster Speedway in 1962.

Jim Bradshaw has built a new racer which will be driven by Bobby Young of Due West tonight. Doris Sosebee will drive the car which Estes raced here last season. Aaron Gailey also has a new racer.

Some other newcomers to the Anderson Speedway tonight include: Jabez Jones, Herman Wise, Tommy Roberts, Lewis Cooper, and Ed Coile.

The program consists of 110 laps of racing in the modified-sportsman, amateur and jalopy division. Races next Friday night will start at 8 o'clock.

LEADERS OF THE PACK . . .

| BUD LUNSFORD | DOUG KENIMER | AARON GAILEY | TOOTLE ESTES |

ANDERSON SPEEDWAY

200-Lap Race Set Here Tonight

All four of the drivers who have won feature races at the Anderson Speedway this season have entered the 200-lap team championship race here tonight.

Tootle Estes of Knoxville, Tenn., has won five features here, Bud Lunsford of Gainesville, Ga., and Aaron Gailey of Lavonia, Ga., each have won four feature races here and Doug Kenimer of Dahlonega, Ga., has won three including a 100-lap championship race.

Jim Bradshaw of Anderson has rebuilt the engine of his car and Tootle Estes will be at its wheel. Estes, Lunsford, Kenimer and Gailey have won the first four spots for tonight's 200-lapper.

Lunsford and Kenimer will be in the front row followed by Estes and Gailey on the second row.

Benny Evatt, winner of the amateur championship race, will team with Lunsford. Jack Henderson, winner of six amateur features, will team with Kenimer. Paul Baker of Greenville will be Estes' teammate. The sportsman drivers who drive cars with wings will be allowed to use them in this race. Modified drivers will use their wings as usual.

Rounding out the top 10 qualifiers are: Jimmy Deason, Greenwood in fifth spot; Steve Chastain of Lavonia, Ga., in 6th place; Charlie Burkhalter of Athens, Ga., 7th; Bobby Christain of Athens, Ga., 8th; Junior Fouche of Athens, Ga., 9th and Marvin Moore of Westminster, 10th.

Only the fastest 20 qualifiers will be allowed to run. Drivers who entered races last week and were unable to qualify will be given a time trial before tonight's race.

Charlie Mize, promoter, explained that since the race will not be stopped except in case a major accident the race should be over much earlier than regular Friday nights' event. A jalopy race will be the other event on the program.

Two separate vacations two persons for three days at two nights at Cadillac Hotel Miami Beach, Fla., will be given away as door prizes at night's race.

Admission is $3 for adults. Children under 12 accompanied by an adult will be admitted free.

'Wings Over Carolina'

Jim Bradberry of Athens, Ga., owns this full-bodied '32 Ford coach which Tootle Estes of Knoxville drives. It's a real hauler and has picked up plenty of prize money at Anderson and Greenwood, S. C., and Banks County, Ga. A fuel-injected Chevy provides the go power.

FREDDIE FRYAR TO RACE HERE
... Skeeter Rocket From Rossville, Ga.

Super Modified 'Skeeter' Races To Be Here Friday

Super modified "skeeter" stock car races will be a special attraction at the Anderson Speedway Friday at 8 p.m.

The "skeeters" have fuel injection engines and burn alcohol for fuel. These are so powerful they must be equipped with a device called "wings" which are mounted on the top of the machines and catch a wind suction forcing the racer to the Speedway. This gives the driver such control that he can go into the turns at top speed.

The "skeeters" are slated to run a 50-lap feature, plus two 10-lap heats. Amateurs and Jalopies will be on the program.

Drivers entered in the "skeeter" division so far: Harold Fryar, Chattanooga, Tenn.; Freddie Fryar, Rossville, Ga.; Leon Sells, Atlanta; Cabbage Pendly, Cumming, Ga.; and Howard Corbin, Chamblee, Ga.

The full-body modifieds will run with the "skeeters" with bonus for the first three finishes.

"Skeeters" To Run Friday Night In Anderson Race

ANDERSON, S.C. — James Bradberry, owner of car no. 6 driven by Tootle Estes says that rain out gave him an extra week to rebuild his racer in a desperate attempt to out run Lunsford Friday at 8 p.m. Bradberry has a complete new racer except for the body. Local racing fans say a car cannot be built that will out run Lunsford, but Estes is out to prove otherwise.

Entries continue to come in for the Super Modified Skeeter Race scheduled for Wednesday, July 3rd at the Anderson Speedway. Drivers entered to date include Harold Fryar, Chattanooga, Tennessee; Leon Sells and Herman Wise, Atlanta; and Jabez Jones from Lavonia.

All driving fuel injection Chevrolets except Jones.

Alcohol is used for fuel in the skeeters entered and each is equipped with wings except Wise who won the race in Atlanta Sunday night. The skeeters have no transmission and are geared straight from engine to the back end. Seven events are on the program which begins at 8:30 p.m. One hundred and ten laps are scheduled plus time trials. The main event will consist of fifty laps. Amateurs are also on the program.

Anderson Speedway is located on Highway 81, the old Anderson-Greenville Road, eleven miles from Anderson, S.C. Admission for this race is $2.50.

HAROLD FYAR, Chattanooga, Tenn., is shown with his "super modified Skeeter" racer which will be in the 100-lap special race program at Anderson Speedway July 3 at 8 p. m. (Special photo.)

ESTES: 'IF YOU WAIT FOR 'BUD' TO MAKE BOO-BOO, YOU'RE LEFT'

By JOHNNY MARTIN
Independent Sports Editor

"Beating Bud Lunsford is like the Mets beating the Yankees," said race-driver Tootle Estes of Knoxville, Tenn. "It doesn't happen very often," he continued.

Lunsford, Gainesville, Ga. driver, won 15 main events in a row at the modified races at Anderson Speedway. Estes was second 12 of those times. It was on Aug. 9 that Estes finally entered the winner's circle at the Anderson oval, called by Estes "the fastest dirt track I run on in four states."

"Lunsford is a good driver and he has a good machine," said Estes. "If you stay behind him and wait for him to make a mistake, you're left. He doesn't make any boo-bos."

Estes, who races in abut 120 main events from mid-April to late-October, says he hopes to give Lunsford a little more competition since he has a more powerful motor.

Estes runs three type of cars —full modified, super modified skeeter, and late model. He prefers the super modified. Two of the three cars are owned by James Bradberry of Athens. "He's the best owner I've ever worked with," Estes commented.

The Tenneessee driver spends more time in cars than he does out of them. For instance, last week he started out with a super modified race at Anderson Speedway Thursday night and followed with a modified race the next night. Last night he raced in a super modified event in Cleveland, Tenn.

Sunday he hopes to make two races—a late model at Dallas, Ga. in the afternoon and a super modified Sunday night at the Peach Bowl in Atlanta. Tuesday night it will be a super modified race in Montgomery, Ala. Next Thursday it will be Greenwood for modified racing, the same at Anderson Friday night, and more modified races at Banks County Speedway in Cornelia Saturday night. Estes says that he will average four events a week and in between races he likes to do a lot of reading.

How much reading can he do in a racing schedule like that?

DOUG KENIMER, right, is shown accepting championship trophy from promoter Charlie Mize, left, after the Georgian won the 100-lap modified championship race at Anderson Speedway Friday night. (Independent Sports Photo by Jack Cromer.)

Here Tonight

LUNSFORD MUST WORK THROUGH TRAFFIC IN QUEST OF NO. 7!

If Gainesville, Ga., race driver Bud Lunsford is to win his 7th main event in a row at Anderson Speedway tonight, he must again work his way through the traffic.

The inverted starts haven't seemed to slow the six - time winner down — but promoters believe it has created considerable excitement as the faster cars battle toward the front.

Tootle Estes of Knoxville, Tenn. will again be out to try and beat the Georgian. Estes has finished second to Lunsford five times. Buck Simmons, 16-year-old whiz, has finished second once, third twice, and fourth once.

The inverted start is scheduled again here tonight at the new Anderson oval for the heat races and main event.

The feature, which will be inverted from last week's finish, calls for Lunsford to start out in the 17th position.

Another large field of amateur drivers are expected, too, with Norman Bowen of Anderson one of the new entries.

The ⅜ of a mile clay speedway has 100 laps of racing tonight on the six-event program for sportsman and amateurs. First race begins at 8 p.m. at the oval located on the old Anderson-Greenville Road, Highway 81, eleven miles from Anderson.

Cars With Air Scoops In Races At Anderson Track

TOMORROW NI
Another Cl
Expected A

Doug Kenimer, a 20-year-old race car driver from Dahlonega, Ga., driving a newly built engine, will return to Anderson Speedway here tomorrow night and attempt to break Buck Simmons' winning streak of two-straight races.

Simmons, of Baldwin, Ga. who recently turned 20, fought a terrific battle to win the last two feature events here and is expected to have another har time tomorrow night.

Two more drivers expected t

Little Buck Simmons, 17-year-old racing demon from Baldwin, Ga., will enter the special races at Anderson Speedway tonight and the Georgian will be driving the car formerly driven by Tootle Estes of Knoxville, Tenn. in the last skeeter race here.

Simmons' car, along with Dub Meeler and Charlie Burkhalter of Athens, Ga. will be equipped with air scoops.

These drivers and others including Allen Williamson, Jabez Jones, Marvin Moore, Floyd Holcombe are expected to increase the main event field to near twenty.

One-hundred-ten laps of racing is scheduled for the seven-event program at Anderson Speedway tonight. Races begin at 8 p. m. with the jalopy event. There will be a 35-lap modified feature, a 20-lap amateur feature and two heat races in that division.

Anderson Speedway is located

BUCK SIMMONS

1.7 miles north of I-85 on Highway 81, between Anderson and Greenville.

RACE HERI

Two
Este:

1965

Bill York and Char halter, two hard luck volved in a mass of wre Anderson Speedway along with Tootle Este been the chief threat to ford's winning streak derson oval, take ai place tonight at the 6-ing program here.

York and Burkhalter much of a chance due

ANDERSON SPEEDWAY
Many Cars To Have New Engines For New Season

Charlie Mize, promoter at Anderson Speedway, says there will be some changes in cars and drivers for the 1965 racing season which opens April 2.

Bud Lunsford of Gainesville, Ga., will have a new machine built from a 1932 Chevy coach body. Doug Kenimer of Dahlonega, Ga., has bought Lunsford's car. Lunsford, who operates a speed shop in Gainesville, has built a new engine for the Kenimer car.

Herman Wise of Atlanta has built a new racer and Billy Smith of Atlanta has purchased the car Wise formerly drove. Smith's car will also have a Lunsford-built engine.

The car driven by Tootle Estes of Knoxville will have a new engine this year. Aaron Gailey of Lavonia will drive the Jim Bradshaw car from Anderson. Guy Tucker of Royston, a newcomer to area racing, will have a racer with a model T body. Steve Chastain, sportsman driver from Lavonia, has moved into the modified division in a car built by Nelson and Grady Ayers.

W. M. Fulmer, sportsman driver from Saluda, has gone modified, too. Bobby Young of Due West and Arnett Autry of Greenwood have purchased the car slated to have been driven by the late Charles Smith of Anderson. Smith was killed in a highway accident in December. Homer Owens, Romey Medlock and Ozark Ike Williams of Duncan plan to run modified cars this year. The drivers formerly drove sportsman cars.

Mize also pointed out that he expects this to be biggest racing year yet for Anderson Speedway fans. "We will have more cars than we have ever had," he said. "We'll have more experienced drivers, and I expect closer races, too."

Skeeter Races Wednesday At Anderson Speedway

Super modified "skeeter" stock car races will be held at the Anderson Speedway Wednesday night at 8:30 p.m.

Wayne McGuire of Grayson, Ky. will drive a fuel-injection Pontiac in the Anderson event. The Kentuckian has won nine races in a row and has been a top driver at many Virginia and Ohio tracks.

Harold Fryar, Chattanooga, Tenn., will be driving the Indianapolis sprint type car owned by Pete Hancock of Athens, Ga.

Buck Simmons, Baldwin, Ga., will drive the James Bradberry car from Athens, Ga., which will be modified with fuel injections and straight drive transmission. Aaron Gailey, Lavonia, Ga., will drive Wendell Roach's car also of Lavonia. Gailey's car will have a new engine.

Bud Lunsford and Doug Kenimer will be running as super modifieds. Other drivers include Herman Wise, Atlanta; Howard Corbin, Buford, Ga.; and Katron Sosebee, Atlanta.

Latest entry for the super modified event is Bill Hemby of Smyrna, Ga. Hemby, a top contender at the Tennessee speedways, will be making his first appearance in Anderson.

The program consists of two 10 lap heats and a 50-lap feature, plus a 15-lap jalopy and a 20-lap amateur race.

Admission will be $2.50. The Anderson Speedway is located 1.7 miles off I-85 on Highway 81 between Anderson and Greenville.

Two free vacations for two for three days and two nights at the Cadillac Hotel in Miami Beach, Fla. will be given away.

AARON GAILEY, shown above, from Lavonia, Ga., who has been a consistent high finisher with only a stock engine in his racer, will be at the Anderson Speedway tonight with his car equipped with a new engine out of the Bud Lunsford Speedshop in Gainesville, Ga.

Can Simmons Make It 4?

Buck Simmons, a racing speed merchant from Baldwin, Ga., had won only one race in four years at Anderson Speedway until three weeks ago.

Since then, Simmons has won three straight feature events and will be trying to make it No. 4 tonight at the Anderson Speedway at 8 p.m.

Simmons has had plenty of competition from many drivers and in particular Doug Kenimer and Steve Chastain. Wilton Watkins, Aaron, Gailey, Jimmy Hall, Jim Deason, and many others are other "drivers to watch", points out promoter Charlie Mize.

The amateur and sportsman divisions have been consolidated to increase the number of cars for the feature event. This also creates a more exciting field of racers and speeds up the time required for the weekly racing program here.

The promoters have promised the track will be in top shape for tonight's events, which will include four heat races and two feature events.

WINNING CAR
Owner James Bradberry of Athens with the winning car in last night's main event at the Anderson Speedway. Tootle Estes piloted the car.

Tootle Estes
NEW WINNER IN MAIN EVENT AT SPEEDWAY

Tootle Estes from Knoxville, Tenn., finally succeeded in outrunning Bud Lunsford, the Gainesville driver who has dominated racing at the Anderson Speedway over the past year.

Estes and Lunsford both won heats to grab the pole positions for last night's main event with Lunsford on the inside and Estes to the outside.

Estes took the lead when the green flag went down and held it by a car length all the way. Lunsford had won last week's

season's opener after winning 18 times on the 3/8 miles oval last year.

Billy Smith of Atlanta finished third and Bobby Young ran fourth in Anderson's Jim Bradshaw's car.

Jim Hall won the amateur main event, trailed by Barry Bagens. Densil Bagwell won the jalopy event.

43

CHAPTER FIVE

HERB "TOOTLE" ESTES AND THE NASCAR YEARS

Over the years many have said, Tootle Estes had the natural ability to race about anything that had four wheels during his long and successful racing career. This included a number of NASCAR races in the old NASCAR Sportsman division; several races in the NASCAR Grand National Series (now the Cup Series); and even a few races in the NASCAR Convertible Series.

On July 1, 1956, Tootle would take another step in his racing career when he entered his first NASCAR Grand National race at the Ashville-Weaverville Speedway. It was car owner Dave Everett who gave Estes a ride in his new 1956 Chevrolet. Tootle started in the 13th starting spot and finished the race in the number 11 position . It was over two years later, on July 30, 1958, before Estes started another Grand National event. This time it was at the Trenton International Speedway in a #30 1957 Ford. Tootle started the race back in the field, but slowly worked his way to a respectful top 15 finish, finishing in 11th place.

Estes' two best finishes in the Grand National Series were two eighth place finishes. One at the Ashville-Weaverville Speedway in a 1958 Ford on June 29, 1958; and the other at Southern States Fairgrounds Speedway in that same 1958 Ford on September 5, 1958. According to family members, the

Tootle Estes in the A.J. King Grand National race car (Photo provided by Bob Markos).

Grand National finish Tootle was the most proud of was his 10th place finish on September 1, 1958 at Darlington International Speedway in the Famed "Southern 500" in 1957 Ford.

Another NASCAR Series, popular among race fans and drivers, from 1956 until its final season in 1962 was the Convertible Division. This series was the NASCAR Series that Tootle enjoyed the most success. In eight races in the series from, his first convertible start at Raleigh (NC) Speedway on July 4,1958; to his last start in this series at Martinsville (VA) Speedway on October 12, 1958, Estes would score 4 top ten finishes. This included a career high second place at Wilson (NC) Speedway in a 1957 Ford convertible on September 7, 1958. In the Wilson race Tootle battled two-time defending Convertible Champion Bob Welborn all the way to the finish line in a very close race (see story at the end of this chapter).

Tootle also had two sixth place finishes within a one week span. The first was at the Greenville-Pickens Speedway on July 19, 1958; and the other sixth place finish was scored at a new dirt track known as the Rambi Raceway on July 26, 1958. The Rambi Raceway would be paved in 1974 and become known as Myrtle Beach Speedway. Both these finishes were in a 1958 Ford convertible #36 (You can see the complete rundown of Estes' Grand National and Convertible races on a chart at the end of this chapter).

Another area of racing that Estes enjoyed great success was in the late model Sportsman division. Tootle also competed in several races in the old NASCAR Sportsman division. During his NASCAR Sportsman days, Estes drove Fords and Mercurys for Woody Bradley. He also drove for Sevierville, Tennessee's, A.J. King in his Dodge Chargers. One of Tootle's best NASCAR Sportsman finishes was a second place finish in a King Dodge. That finish was scored in the Blount 300 at the Smokey Mountain Speedway. Chattanooga's Bob Burcham won the race followed closely by Estes. However, over the years, most of his wins in the late model sportsman division came in regional races between the late 1950's until the late '60's.

During the mid-70's Estes made two attempts to qualify for NASCAR's Permatex 300 in Bradley's 1969 Mercury. This race ran from 1966 until it was changed to the NASCAR Xfinity Series in 1982. Over the years the race was also sponsored by Goody's, the headache powder company.

Estes had a number of late model sportsman wins all over the Southeast from the start of the '60's until the mid-70's. He won races at Newport (TN) Speedway, Corbin (KY) Speedway, and several other Southern tracks. According to Wayne Wells, who was the engine builder for Bradley's race cars from 1966

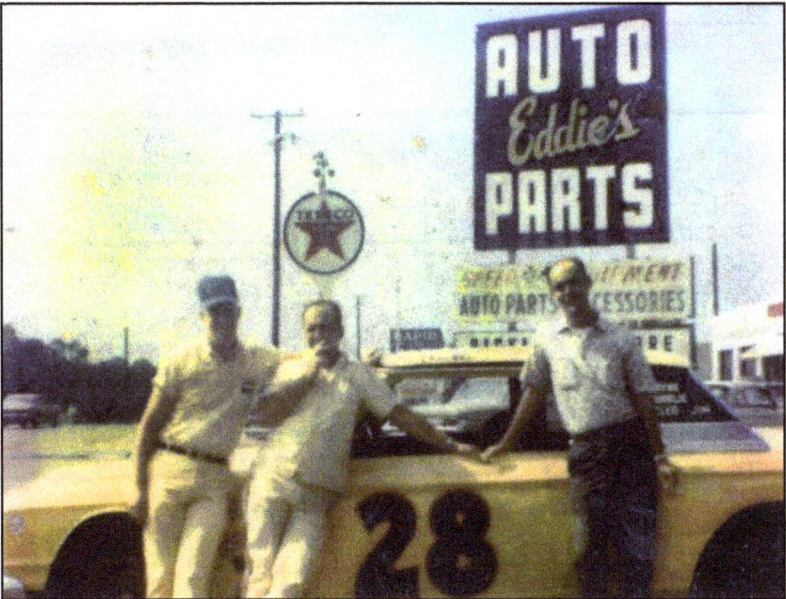

Wayne Wells, second from the left, stands beside one of my all-time favorite race cars. That is the Woody Bradley yellow #28 Ford Fairlane. Fred Henry is on the right. He was the manager of Woody's Auto Parts (Photo provided by Wayne Wells).

to 1974, Tootle had some of his best years in the sportsman ranks at the Smoky Mountain Speedway; the legendary half mile dirt track located near Maryville, Tennessee. He won a number of feature races at this track over some of the best sportsman drivers in the South such as, Bob Burcham, Jack Ingram, Joe Lee Johnson, L.D. Ottinger, Wes Williams, and others. He also scored a big win at Newport (TN) Speedway in a 300 lap sportsman race over hometown driver, Wes Williams.

Wayne Wells told me in an interview, "One of the most unique sponsors that Tootle had during his career was Don Cameron, President of the big Millers Department Store in downtown Knoxville. Cameron's eleven year old son was a big Tootle Estes fan. So to make his son feel a part of the Estes team, he sponsored Tootle at many of the Knoxville area races, especially those at Smoky Mountain Speedway."

As the 1970's dawned on the racing world, the sportsman cars were losing their popularity. It was now late model racing that was about to become the major division for racing, especially dirt racing. Race teams and drivers alike started to focus on what would become the most popular form of short track racing in the country.

By the late 1970's the dirt late model division was preparing to explode onto the national scene; as a promoter, years ahead of his time, by the name of Robert Smawley was poised to bring dirt racing into the modern era. He nationalized the sport and its drivers, making national stars out of regional drivers; he paid unheard of $10,000 to win purses; and he introduced new ideas to the sport like, Series Driver Championships, and souvenir trailers for the race fans.

Late model racing has become the signature division for short track racing throughout the country. This is clearly seen by how quickly the cars have evolved through the years.

Gary L. Parker

Date	Place	Division	Start	Finish	Owner	#	Car	Laps	Money	Status	Laps Led
Jul 1 1956	Asheville-Weaverville Speedway	NASCAR Grand National	13	11	Dave Everett	100	1956 Chevrolet	178	100	running	
May 30 1958	Trenton International Speedway	NASCAR Grand National	30	11	Tootle Estes	30	1957 Ford	457	425	running	0
Jun 15 1958	Reading Fairgrounds	NASCAR Grand National	19	30	Tootle Estes	30	1957 Ford	11		brakes	0
Jun 29 1958	Asheville-Weaverville Speedway	NASCAR Grand National	6	8		16	1958 Ford	192	150	running	0
Jul 4 1958	Raleigh Speedway	NASCAR Grand National/Convertible	55	44	Tootle Estes	36	1958 Ford	85		engine	0
Jul 19 1958	Greenville-Pickens Speedway	NASCAR Convertible	6	6	Herbert Estes	36	1958 Ford Convertible	193	200	running	
Jul 26 1958	Rambi Raceway	NASCAR Convertible	1	6	Herbert Estes	36	1958 Ford Convertible	191	200	running	
Aug 7 1958	Columbia Speedway	NASCAR Grand National	5	15	Tootle Estes	36	1958 Ford	130	70	spindle	
Aug 8 1958	Southern States Fairgrounds	NASCAR Convertible	8	14	Herbert Estes	36	1958 Ford Convertible	104	85	accident	
Aug 10 1958	Music City Motorplex	NASCAR Grand National/Convertible	21	9	Tootle Estes	36	1958 Ford Convertible	192	250	running	0
Aug 17 1958	Asheville-Weaverville Speedway	NASCAR Grand National/Convertible	19	28	Tootle Estes	36	1958 Ford	181	100	steering	
Sep 1 1958	Darlington Raceway	NASCAR Grand National	21	10	Tootle Estes	36	1957 Ford	346	675	running	0
Sep 5 1958	Southern States Fairgrounds	NASCAR Grand National	20	8	Tootle Estes	36	1958 Ford	176	150	running	0
Sep 7 1958	Wilson Speedway	NASCAR Convertible	6	2	Herbert Estes	36	1957 Ford Convertible	150	525	running	
Sep 12 1958	Gastonia Fairgrounds	NASCAR Grand National	6	16	Tootle Estes	36	1958 Ford	102	60	valve	
Oct 12 1958	Martinsville Speedway	NASCAR Grand National/Convertible	36	19	Tootle Estes	36	1958 Ford	330	165	running	0

49

Grand National Race No. 41
364 Laps at Darlington Raceway
Darlington, SC
"Southern 500"
500 Miles on 1.375-Mile Paved Track
September 1, 1958

Fin	St	No.	Driver	Team / Car	Laps	Money	Status
1	2	22	Fireball Roberts	Frank Strickland '57 Chevrolet	364	$13,220	Running
2	7	87	Buck Baker	Baker '57 Chevrolet	359	5,750	Running
3	8	99	Shorty Rollins	Rollins '58 Ford	359	3,615	Running
4	17	46	Speedy Thompson	Thompson '57 Chevrolet	358	1,995	Running
5	20	98	Marvin Panch	John Whitford '58 Ford	357	1,525	Running
6	25	49	Bob Welborn	Julian Petty '57 Chevrolet	355	1,150	Running
7	13	40	Rex White	'58 Chevrolet	348	1,045	Running
8	34	30	Doug Cox	'57 Ford	348	925	Running
9	23	95	Bob Duell	Julian Buesink '57 Ford	346	775	Running
10	21	36	Herb Estes	Estes '57 Ford	346	675	Running
11	28	11	Junior Johnson	Paul Spaulding '57 Ford	345	500	Running
12	33	66	Roy Tyner	A M Crawford '58 Plymouth	344	400	Running
13	29	92	Wilbur Rakestraw	'57 Ford	344	300	Running
14	19	1	Speedy Thompson	'58 Chevrolet	344	310	Running
15	30	44	Lloyd Dane	'57 Ford	343	250	Running
16	12	86	G C Spencer	'57 Chevrolet	343	315	Running
17	35	48	Possum Jones	Julian Petty '57 Chevrolet	342	225	Running
18	22	97	Parnelli Jones	Vel's '57 Ford	340	200	Running
19	5	42	Lee Petty	Petty Engineerin g'57 Olds	335	345	Running
20	36	25	Gene White	White '57 Chevrolet	328	200	Running
21	31	15	Jim Paschal	'57 Chevrolet	321	150	Engine
22	10	19	Herman Beam	Beam '57 Chevrolet	311	190	Running
23	15	77	Bobby Johns	Shorty Johns '57 Chevrolet	304	150	Engine
24	18	88	Tiny Lund	Jim Linke '58 Ford	285	230	Running
25	41	94	Clarence DeZalia	DeZalia '56 Ford	277	150	Running
26	48	33	Al White	'58 Ford	264	100	Running
27	43	85	Carl Tyler	Tyler '57 Ford	248	100	Running
28	27	2	Bobby Lee	Horne Motors '58 Ford	230	100	Running
29	3	12	Joe Weatherly	Holman - Moody '58 Ford	226	265	Engine
30	45	74	L D Austin	Austin '57 Ford	214	100	Running
31	14	47	Jack Smith	Smith '58 Pontiac	210	100	Crash
32	16	43	Jim Reed	Petty Engineering '57 Olds	207	315	Engine
33	4	26	Curtis Turner	Holman - Moody '58 Ford	195	1,350	Engine
34	24	8	Eddie Gray	Vel's '57 Ford	180	100	Crash
35	6	6	Joe Eubanks	Cotton Owens '57 Pontiac	146	380	Clutch
36	1	45	Eddie Pagan	Pagan '58 Ford	136	240	Crash
37	47	9	Jesse James Taylor	Jesse James '56 Ford	95	100	Crash
38	38	89	Marvin Porter	'57 Ford	92	100	Crash
39	11	24	Larry Frank	'57 Chevrolet	71	275	Crash
40	32	14	George Dunn	Manley Britt '57 Mercury	61	100	Engine
41	27	10	Reds Kagle	Kagle '57 Ford	49	100	Piston
42	26	90	Emanuel Zervakis	Junie Donlavey '57 Chevy	47	100	Heating
43	46	5	Cotton Owens	'57 Dodge	15	100	Piston
44	42	31	Bob Bolheimer	Monroe Shook '58 Chevy	15	100	Heating
45	44	81	Harvey Hege	Hege '57 Ford	8	100	Throttle
46	39	60	Don Kimberling	'58 Chevrolet	7	100	Crash
47	9	55	Jimmy Massey	Brushy Mt. Motors '57 Pontiac	5	100	Trans
48	40	84	Bob Perry	'57 Ford	1	100	Engine

Time of Race: 4 hours, 52 minutes, 44 seconds.
Average Speed: 102.585 mph
Pole Winner: Eddie Pagan - 116.952 mph
Fastest Qualifier: Fireball Roberts - 118.648 mph
Lap Leaders: Joe Weatherly 1, Eddie Pagan 2-12, Joe Eubanks 13-38, Curtis Turner 39-85, Pagan 86-87, Speedy Thompson 88-93, Turner 94-168, Fireball Roberts 169-364.
Cautions: 6 for 28 laps
Margin of Victory: 5-laps-plus
Attendance: 80,000

Convertible Race No. 18
150 Laps at Wilson Speedway
Wilson, NC
75 Miles on Half-mile Dirt Track
September 7, 1958

Fin	St	No.	Driver	Team / Car	Laps	Money	Status
1	2	49	Bob Welborn	J H Petty '57 Chevrolet	150	$800	Running
2	6	36	Herb Estes	Estes '57 Ford	150	525	Running
3	14	32	Brownie King	Jess Potter '57 Chevrolet	149	360	Running
4	4	14	George Dunn	Manley Britt '57 Mercury	149	250	Running
5	11	42	Richard Petty	Petty Eng '57 Oldsmobile	149	225	Running
6	9	53	Doug Yates	'57 Chevrolet	149	200	Running
7	13	52	Bob Walden	'57 Ford	149	195	Running
8	10	41	Whitey Norman	'57 Chevrolet	148	150	Running
9	12	76	Larry Frank	Frank '57 Chevrolet	148	140	Running
10	7	58	Bill Morton	James Lowery '57 Ford	148	135	Running
11	3	74	L D Austin	Austin '56 Chevrolet	146	125	Running
12	15	66	Roy Tyner	Spook Crawford '58 Plymouth	146	110	Running
13	8	8	Elmo Langley	'57 Chevrolet	144	100	Running
14	16	711	Bill Poor	Poor '56 Chevrolet	143	85	Running
15	23	81	Harvey Hege	'57 Ford	139	70	Running
16	21	94	Neil Castles	Clarence DeZalia '56 Ford	137	60	Running
17	19	19	Shep Langdon	'56 Ford	132	50	Running
18	22	18	Dick Walters	'56 Ford	129	50	Running
19	5	97	Barney Shore	Shore '57 Chevrolet	123	50	Crash
20	18	202	Johnny Gardner	'56 Ford	122	50	Running
21	20	67	Vernon Vest	'56 Dodge	120	50	Running
22	17	17	Fred Harb	Harb '57 Mercury	60	50	Radiator
23	1	44	Ken Rush	J H Petty '57 Chevrolet	11	50	Crash

Time of Race: 1 hour, 39 minutes, 34 seconds
Average Speed: 45.196 mph
Pole Winner: Ken Rush - 58.046 mph
Lap Leaders: Bob Welborn -150.
Cautions: Margin of Victory: Attendance: 4,300

Welborn Waxes Wilson Field For 7th of Year

WILSON, NC (Sept. 7) -- Bob Welborn scooted around Ken Rush's early wreck and drove his Chevrolet to victory in the 75-miler at Wilson Speedway. It was the seventh win of the season for the two-time defending Convertible champion.

Welborn's triumph put him 862 points ahead of Larry Frank in the chase for the 1958 Ragtop title with only one Convertible race and a pair of Sweepstakes events left of the schedule.

Welborn nosed out Herb Estes for the $800 top prize on the gently banked half-mile dirt track. Brownie King posted his best career finish by taking third place. George Dunn came in fourth and young Richard Petty fifth. It was Petty's first top five finish of his career.

Rush and Welborn started on the front row in Chevrolets owned and prepared by J.H. "Julian" Petty. Rush took the lead at the outset, but was involved in a crash on lap 11.

Barney Shore qualified a surprising fifth, but crashed his Chevrolet on lap 123.

L.D. Austin started third on the grid, but fell back to an 11th place finish in his two year old Chevrolet.

Tootle Estes

Date	Place	Division	Start	Finish	Owner	#	Car	Laps	Money	Status	Laps Led
Nov 1 1970	Smoky Mountain Raceway	NASCAR Late Model Sportsman		2			1967 Dodge	300	975	running	
Nov 8 1970	Martinsville Speedway	NASCAR Late Model Sportsman		6			1967 Dodge Charger	245	400		
May 14 1972	Smoky Mountain Raceway	NASCAR Grand National East	27	17	Tootle Estes	71	1969 Ford	120	225	rear end	0

51

Burcham Sets Pace To Win Blount 300

MARYVILLE, Tenn. — Bob Burcham outdistanced the opposition Sunday afternoon at the Smokey Mountain Raceway here, to win the annual Blount 300 NASCAR late model sportsman national championship stock car race.

Driving a 1964 Chevelle, Burcham took the lead on the tenth lap and was only out of first place briefly for a quick pit stop. The Chattanooga driver averaged 70.96 miles per hour around the half-mile paved track and completed the 300 laps in two hours, 11 minutes and 54 seconds.

Tootles Estes finished second in a 197 Dodge, followed by Bosco Lowe in a 1965 Chevelle ,Al Grinnan in a 1967 Chevelle and Joe Thurman in a 195 Chevelle.

The victory was worth $1,-600 for Burcham. Estes took home $975 for second place.

The race was slowed eight times by the yellow caution flag, for a total of 70 laps. On the 187th lap, defending national champion Charles (Red) Farmer, running second, L. D. Ottinger, running third, Paul Lewis and Darrel Waltrip all demolished their cars in a grinding crash. Luckily, there were no injuries.

Children's Brick 200 Bo

secial To The Journal
MARYVILLE, Sept. 21—More nan 30 of the greatest Sports- 1an drivers from the South will e matched Saturday night dur- ig the running of the Children's rick 200 at Smoky Mountain aceway.

Action is scheduled to begin t 8:30 p.m. on the high banks ! SMR's one-half mile dirt val. "This is probably the reatest race ever to be sched- led at Smoky Mountain Race- ay and we are paying the ighest purse in our three year ssociation with NASCAR" pro- toter Don Naman said.

Tickets are on sale for $5 ach. "Children's Hospital will e the big champion," Naman aid. SMR is donating $1 from he sale of every ticket to the ast Tennessee Children's Hos- ital Brick Campaign which is ow in progress. "Your ticket vill bring one of the best shows ver in automobile racing plus he extra benefit of a $1 dona- ion to the ETCH $3,000,000 uilding fund," Naman said.

A purse of $5650 is being of- ered to Sportsman and Hobby 'ar drivers. Winner of the 100- nile Sportsman race will col- ect $1200. As an added attrac- ion a special 50-lap Hobby race

Curtis Turner, one of the greatest racing drivers ever to compete on the NASCAR circuit, has entered the Chil- dren's Buick 200 and will drive a new 61 Ford owned by Lin Easterland of Savannah, Ga. Turner, inventor of the dirt track power slide, had this to say about the race: "I am going to put on a show for you fans at SMR and you can bet the car will be running full bore." Fred Langley, at East Tennessee Ford, is re- sponsible for Turner's ap- pearance at the benefit race.

s scheduled, and these drivers eally go for the checkered flag.
Jim Hunter, former t r a c k :hampion, is returning to action ifter a few weeks' layoff. Hunt- :r, who will be at the wheel of is former No. 85 Chevrolet Chevelle, is driving for a new :ar owner and must be con- sidered a top candidate for vic- ory lane.

"There are close to 20 auto- mobiles that could take the :heckered flag. This race should be one of the most competitive aysr ran at SMR," Naman said. Toodle Estes, current point

Johnson   Pistone   Lewis   Lund   Moore   Hunter

leader from Knoxville, has a fine season of victories to his credit. Estes drives a 64 Ford Fairlane and won the Trenton 100 and Victory 200 this year.

Other top drivers i n c l u d e Knoxville's Joe Ed Neubert, who will be wheeling a 64 Chev- elle owned by Kenneth Young of Maryville, Joe Thurman, of Rocky Mount, Va., who is pres- ently holding second place in National Sportsman's standings and drives a 64 Chevelle, plus Grand National circuit drivers Tiny Lund and Tiger Tom Pistone.

Lund will be wheeling a new 61 Ford and Pistone will be piloting a 64 Ford. Joe Lee Johnson, from Chattanooga and

one of the winningest drivers at SMR, will be on hand in his red and black 63 Ford.

Bud Moore, who must be con- sidered the hottest driver now on the Grand National Circuit, from Charlotte, N. C., is en- tered in a 64 Chevelle. Moore placed fifth at Darlington and Atlanta this season driving a 67 Dodge Charger owned by John- son City's A. J. King. Moore has plenty of dirt track ex- perience and drives like he's hungry for victory.

Paul Lewis, a winner at SMR last year after beating the field in the annual Grand National Smoky 200, will be wheeling a 55 Chevy. Lewis says his car is "running great" and should be

CURTIS TURNER

considered a top contender.

The following have submitted entries for Saturday nights race:
Tiny Lund, Cross, S. C., 61 Ford.
Toodle Estes, Knoxville, 64 Ford Fairlane.
Andy Buffington, Atlanta, Ga., 56 Chevy.
Charles McKenzie, Atlanta, Ga., 63 Ford.
George Gosnell, Hendersonville, N.C., 63 Plymouth.
Leon Sells, Atlanta, Ga., 64 Chevelle.
Charlie Stone, Atlanta, Ga., 64 Chevelle.
Paul Ghose, Morristown, 55 Chevy.
Joe Ed Neubert, Knoxville, 64 Chevelle.
Herman Goddard, Knoxville, 59 Chevy.
Bud Moore, Charlotte, N.C., 64 Chevelle.
Joe Lee Johnson, Chattanooga, 63 Ford.
Walt Ball, Johnson City, 56 Chevy.
Charlie Smelcer, Morristown, 59 Ford.
Stu McMahan, Dandridge, 61 Ford.
Bill McMahan, Dandridge, 62 Mercury.
Henk Maxwell, Newport, 55 Chevy.
Roger Tunnell, Bristol, 56 Chevy.
Chet Williams, Morristown, 64 Chevelle.
Billy Smith, Asheville, N.C., 56 Ford.
Tom Pistone, Charlotte, N.C., 64 Ford.
Jim Hunter, Knoxville, 64 Chevelle.
Paul Lewis, Johnson City, 55 Chevy.
Andy Petley, Dalton, Ga., 63 Ford.

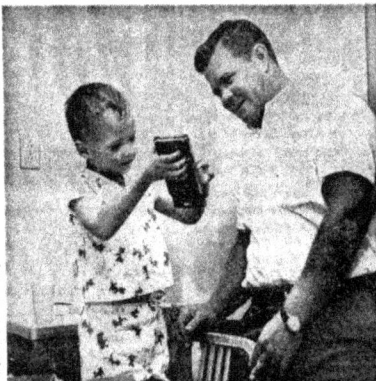

—Staff photo by Al Roberts
RACE TALK — Toodle Estes, one of the favorites in Saturday night's Children's Brick 200 at Smoky Mountain Raceway, takes time out to talk racing with four-year-old Charles W. Hall Jr., at Children's Hospital yesterday. Estes, a consistant winner in Knoxville's racing circuit, will be driving a '64 Ford Fairlane in the big race at Maryville.

Estes To Challenge Big D Once Again

By BILL LUTHER
News-Sentinel Sports Writer

No one can say that Woody Bradley and Tootle Estes are quitters. Bradley, the car builder, and Estes, the driver, know what it's like to not make the race.

But, they're going to try again.

Bradley's 1969 Mercury is among the early entries for the $72,700 Permatex 300 next month at Daytona International Speedway. Estes is tabbed to drive.

"I'll never show up at this speedway again without a car I know will make the field," said a disgusted Estes last February in the garage at Daytona. "It's useless to come here without a car you know will run. The competition is too tough."

Apparently, Estes and Bradley have the Mercury ready to go. Otherwise, Tootle, if he meant what he said, wouldn't be going back.

Three other East Tennessee drivers have filed for the Permatex.

They are reigning national late model sportsman champ L.D. Ottinger and Randy Bethea, both of Newport, and Larry Utsman of Bluff City.

Ottinger, who ran away with the 1975 title, probably won't make a decision on whether to make another championship bid until the Daytona event. That's the spot where the top contenders do just that.

Ottinger and Utsman, who made his first start at Big D last year, will be in Chevelles, Bethea in a Ford.

Morgan Shepard of Conover, N.C., was unable challenge Ottinger in 1975 after Tiny Lund, L.D.'s closest pursuer, was killed at Talladega, Ala. L.D. totaled 9417 points. Shepard took second with 7580. Another Tennessean, Brad Teague of Johnson City, ranked 17th.

The Permatex 300 will be worth $16,000 to the victor. A field of more than 80 drivers will be trying for a berth in the 40-car lineup.

Jack Ingram, three-time national

Estes   Bradley

champ from North Carolina, will defend his 300 crown. Grand National regular Lennie Pond also has filed entry.

Speed Weeks, which comprise more than two weeks of action at Daytona, open Jan. 31 with the 24 Hours of Daytona. When the checkered flag falls for the Daytona 500 on Feb. 15, $815,000 — an increase of $175,000 over 1975 — will have been earned.

The 24 Hours of Daytona should be more attractive to fans in the South since Grand National cars will be eligible. Benny Parsons, winner of the Daytona 500 last February, will team with England's David Hobbs in a BMW for the opening event.

Speedway officials expect five or six GN cars. The 24 Hours run, which is broken down into classes, offers a $10,000 purse for the top GN finisher.

Parsons and Hobbs will run as teammates in the 500 — both in Chevrolets. Buddy Baker (Ford), David Pearson (Mercury) and Pond (Chevrolet) have filed entries. Such stars as Richard Petty (Dodge), Dave Marcis (Dodge), Bobby Allison (Mercury) and Darrell Waltrip (Chevrolet) will be in the lineup.

THE 500, richest ever with a purse of $322,000, gives a driver a shot at a possible $56,500 total take. It'll be possible for the runnerup to pocket $40,000.

Gary L. Parker

CHAPTER SIX

THE SPORTSMAN BECOMES THE LATE MODEL

At the end of the 1960's "Sportsman" race cars became known, to both race fans and drivers alike, as "Late Models." This was a more modern sounding term and was really where this racing division was evolving. Most of the race cars were "home built" stock appearing 1955-56 Fords and Chevrolets. However, by the mid-60's, Chevy Chevelles and Ford Fairlanes would start to replace the earlier versions of the Late Model. Finally, as the late 1970's approached the smaller Camaros, Firebirds, and Mustangs would become the dominant type

Tootle Estes' Ford Mustang. Standing by the car left to right are, Lee Quinton, Wayne Wells, Woody Bradley, and John Kelley (Photo provided by Wayne Wells).

Estes (far right) looks on as a tire is changed on his A.J. King Dodge Charger (Photo from a Smoky Mountain Speedway racing program).

of Late Models found throughout the country. These smaller race cars were made popular by a new national dirt racing series known as the National Dirt Racing Association (NDRA).

The modified and super modified skeeters had enjoyed the main stage of popularity throughout most of the '60's. As we have seen, Estes scored his fair share of wins in both modifieds and skeeters across much of the Southeast.

I last saw the skeeters race at the Rome (GA) Speedway during the late 1960's. That race was won by one of Tootle's biggest rivals, Bud Lunsford. Estes, like most of the other drivers, had already left the modified ranks and were now racing late models. This became the most popular form of dirt racing as the '70's dawned on the sport. In large part, the popularity of the late model was due to its street appearing look. Race fans could identify with these race cars because they looked like the cars they were driving. I think the declining interest in modifieds was the result of two main reasons. First, their look was not the look of something you could drive on the street. And secondly, the cost had become too much for a lot of race teams to justify. In other words, too much money spent versus the money won.

The sportsman cars had raced throughout the 1950's and into the '60's in many parts of the country. As mentioned earlier, NASCAR had a sportsman division for many years. Drivers like, Tootle Estes. Jack Ingram, Jim Hunter, L.D. Ottinger, Joe Ed Nubert, Tiny Lund, Curtis Turner, and many others made a name for themselves in this division. Estes drove several years in the sportsman ranks for Knoxville, Tennessee's Woody

Tootle Estes takes a win at the Corbin (KY) Speedway in the Paul's Auto Parts #6 race car (Photo provided by Tommy Hickman).

Estes poses beside the Danny Evans Masters Touch Coiffeurs #6 race car (Photo provided by Wayne Wells).

Bradley, owner of Woody's Auto Clinic. Most of the engine work was done by Wayne Wells, and the body work was handled by Charlie Young. Among the cars he drove for Woody were, the yellow #28 Ford Fairlane (mentioned in the introduction) and a very good looking Ford Mustang 2+2 #28. Estes had a lot of success with Bradley and won a number of races all over the South at tracks like, Corbin (KY) Speedway, Newport (TN) Speedway, Smoky Mountain Speedway, and the Knoxville (TN) Raceway.

Another sportsman car owner that Estes drove for was Sevierville, Tennessee's A.J King in one of his Dodge race car's. The car was a blue Dodge Charger that had once been driven by Lee Roy Yarbrough. It was in an A.J. King Dodge that Tiny Lund was killed in at Talladega Super Speedway on August 17, 1975. It was probably no fault of the car, as Lund was hit in the driver's door during a multi-car pileup.

As the 1970's approached, Estes began driving late model race cars full time. This would be where he would make yet another name for himself as one of the best late model drivers in the South. During his late model career Estes drove for a number of car owners. Among those were, West Haven Auto Parts owner, the late Herman Collins; Knoxville's Bill Ogle, Sr., a former owner of both Atomic (TN) Speedway and Smoky Mountain Speedway; Knoxville, Tennessee's Danny Evans owner of Master's Touch Coiffeurs; Paul Hickman, owner of Paul's Auto Parts located in Soddy-Daisy, Tennessee; and Ralph Curtis owner of Curtis Equipment Company, located in Loudon, Tennessee.

Paul's son, Tommy, who now runs Paul's Auto Parts said, "Tootle raced for us for a number of years beginning in the early '70's." Tommy said, "We won a lot of races all over the South at tracks like, Atomic (TN) Speedway; 411 Speedway near Seymour, Tennessee; Corbin (KY) Speedway on the Asphalt; Newport (TN) Speedway; Boyd's Speedway near

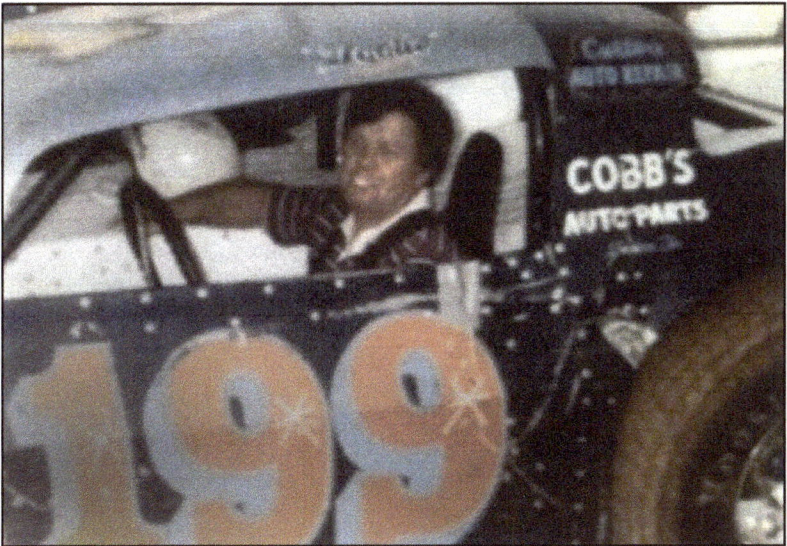

Tootle in the Curtis Equipment #199 before the start of a race (Photo provided by Rocky Estes).

Ringgold, Georgia; the Davy Crockett Speedway in Rogersville, Tennessee; at a number of tracks in South Carolina; and even in Alabama at the big 5/8th mile Gadsden Speedway."

Tommy went on to say, "Gadsden was one of the biggest and fastest tracks we raced on. It was very fast with speeds well over a 100 mph average. One day Tootle showed up late for a race wearing a very ragged button up shirt. Tommy began smiling as he told what happened next, "I asked him if he wanted another shirt and he said no. So he climbed in and was starting on the pole. The green flag dropped and old Tootle went off and hide from the field." He started to laugh as he told what happened then, "As Tootle started going by the pits, I would see little pieces of something flying out the windows. I kept seeing this the whole race." Tommy was laughing very hard as he told me, "When he pulled in after winning the race, I knew what it was that was flying out the window. It was Tootle's shirt coming apart because of the speed. All he had left was the sleeves and the row of buttons."

Later, Hickman said, "A driver by the name of Don Gibbs had been the man to beat at Gadsden for a while. So the track promoter started giving us some 'Show Money' to come and try and out run Gibbs." Tommy then said, "All the drivers were trying to see if we were being paid this 'Show Money.' Well at the driver's meeting all eyes were on us, to see if we were indeed getting this money. The promoter always gave the drivers popcorn during the meeting." Hickman went on with a laugh, "Guess where the promoter was hiding the $100 money he gave us? It was in the popcorn. No one ever caught on."

Hickman later said, "We won seven in a row during one streak at Gadsden. We also won a lot of races at 411 Speedway." Tommy said in closing, "We would win at 411 during one period, but would always end up running second at Atomic, most times behind H.E. Vineyard. But after he won his first race at Atomic he was a frequent winner after that."

Over his career in the late model ranks, one of Tootle's favorite people to drive for was the Late Herman Collins. He drove off and on for Collins for a number of years. He drove a Collins car in some of Robert Smawley's early NDRA races at Atomic and the Volunteer Speedways. Herman said of Estes in a newspaper article one time, "Tootle Estes was the best driver there ever was, period. He was good in any kind of race car he ran and he won around 1200 races in all kinds of race cars."

Estes also had success driving the Masters Touch Coiffeurs #6 blue and gold Chevy II of Danny Evans. Tootle won a number of races for Evans all over the region at tracks that included the now historic Atomic (TN) Speedway. However, Danny Evans biggest win came at an NDRA race at the Volunteer Speedway on June 9, 1979. Another Knoxville driver by the name of H.E. Vineyard would score that victory in the Looney Chevrolet 100, taking the $10,000 win in a thrilling finish over the soon to be legendary dirt warrior, Buck Simmons.

During his career, Tootle won several late model track championships that included three titles at Atomic (TN) Speedway and one at Volunteer Speedway at Bull's Gap, Tennessee in 1980. Estes also won two NASCAR Sportsman titles at one of his favorite tracks, Smoky Mountain Speedway. Tootle won a number of races over the years at Smoky Mountain in both sportsman and late model race cars.

According to many who followed Estes' late model career, he won between 300 and 400 late model races. A few of his major late model wins include, the 1974 "Firecracker 75" at Gadsden, Alabama; Three big wins at another of his favorite tracks, Atomic (TN) Speedway. They included, the "Dogwood

Arts 100," taking the lead from Joe Lee Johnson on lap 31 and leading the rest of the way in his #6 Chevelle over second place finisher Snooks DeFoor in a Ford Mustang; the "Hall of Fame 200" in 1975; and the "Tennessee/Atomic State Championship" race. In 1980 he won the "Jerry's Automotive/Volunteer 100" at the Volunteer Speedway at Bull's Gap, Tennessee. In this race, Estes took the West Haven Auto Parts #6 to the front on lap 97, after starting eight. He won the race over Dayton, Ohio's Don Seaborn.

The last person Estes drove for was Ralph Curtis, owner of Curtis Equipment out of nearby Loudon, Tennessee. Tootle drove the now famous #199, winning a number of races in what he called, "The best race car I ever sat down in."

On August 20, 1982 Tootle Estes would win his last race in this car. More about that in the next chapter.

Tootle Estes First In Volunteer Automotive 100

BY PAUL MCLAIN
Morristown, Tenn.

BULLS GAP, Tenn. (Oct. 12)— A veteran of many years on the Southern dirt tracks, Tootle Estes of Knoxville won the Jerry's Automotive 100 today at Volunteer Speedway and took home the $2,000 first-place money.

Driving the West Haven Auto Parts #6 Camaro owned by Herman Collins, Estes took the lead on the 97th lap of the 100-lap feature to take the checkered flag. Estes started the event in the eighth position and had worked his way up to second behind Ronnie Johnson, who was leading at that point. But mechanical problems forced Johnson to the pits within three laps remaining and moved Estes into the lead.

This was the second time at Volunteer this year that Johnson had been less than five laps away from a $2,000 win only to have a broken wrist pits cost him the victory. Johnson had taken the lead from fastest qualifier Don Seaborn (15.06 seconds) on the third lap and had the strongest car in the field, as he was lapping cars with ease until his trouble.

Coming in second was Seaborn of Dayton, Ohio, in the #74 A.J. Stapleton Excavating

Camaro. After the race, Seaborn stated, "Even though the number 6 was in front of me at the finish, I feel that I won the race because he (Estes) had been put behind me on a restart and was a lap down. I wasn't even running hard to try and pass him."

A recheck of the scorers' check showed that the finish would stand. "I knew all along I had it won," said Estes.

Taking third was Knoxville's H.E. Vineyard, driving David Wagner's #124 Camaro. Fourth went to Herman Goddard of Knoxville in his #22 Dillon chassis Camaro. L.D. Ottinger of Newport took fifth in the #00 Pools Camaro.

Sixth through ninth were Bob Street of Johnson City, Delmas Conley of Portsmouth, Ohio, Ernest King of Johnson City and Rick Rogers of Knoxville.

Johnson, of Chattanooga, wound up 10th, as he did in the Memorial Day 100.

Freddy Smith of Kings Mountain, N.C., had qualified his #00 in second but tire problems during the early portion of the race forced him to retire early, dropping him to 20th place.

The top four finishers in the Late Model consolation made the 100-lapper. Hawkeye

Hawkins won the consolation, with Lamar Winkel, Bill DeGroat and Joe Sams following him across the line.

Buzz Collins of Greeneville won the 25-lap Six-Cylinder special event worth $600. Starting in the front row beside fastest qualifier David Bundren, Collins put his #47 Maverick into the lead on the first lap and led all the way to take the checkered

and first-place money. Bundren fell out with mechanical problems during the race.

Taking second was Richie Lovell from Newport, third went to Matt Seals of Morristown, fourth to John Doty and fifth to Eddie Northern.

Tommy Morrow of Newport won the Bomber feature, with Lewis Hickey of Morristown second. Glen Hughes took the

Mini-Stock feature.

Jerry's Automotive 100 Feature Finish:
1. Tootle Estes; 2. Don Seaborn; 3. H.E. Vineyard; 4. Herman Goddard; 5. L.D. Ottinger; 6. Bob Street; 7. Delmas Conley; 8. Ernest King; 9. Rick Rogers; 10. Ronnie Johnson; 11. Joe Richey; 12. James Hartman; 13. Darrell Monk; 14. Danny Burke; 15. Lamar Winkle; 16. Joe Sams; 17. Hawkeye Hawkins; 18. Bill DeGroat; 19. Mike Clonce; 20. Freddy Smith; 21. Bill Ogle; 22. Rusty Wilson; 23. Jack Pennington; 24. Bill Daum.

Buzz Collins took yet another checkered flag in the Six-Cylinder division as he won the special event for that class at Volunteer Speedway on October 12. (Tommy Guy photo)

Gary L. Parker

Estes Wins Two Straight At Gasden Raceway

Glencoe,Ala.(July 6) - In the fast Modified main event held Saturday night at Gadsden Raceway, Tootle Estes (Knoxville, Tenn.) charged to victory and made it two in a row at the fast 5/8-mile clay oval. Three weeks ago Estes came in second in his first visit to the track.

Leon Brindle (Dalton, Ga.) finished second after Gene Cline (Rome) went out of the race near the end with a blown engine. Garner Snowden (Rome) was a close third, and rounding positions four through eight were Max Scott (Rome), Kenneth Orr (Newnan), Fred Cook (Cleveland, Tenn.), Wayne Nash (Blountsville, Ala.), and Wayne Cavender (Carrolton, Ga.).

In the $200-to win Hobby division Special, Shug Willingham (Pell City, Ala.) came in first, just as he had done for the four previous weeks in regular races.

Stud Dearman (Talladega) and Jerry

Atomic's Dogwood Dinero to Estes

KNOXVILLE, Tenn. — Chevelle - mounted Tootle Estes started Saturday night's Dogwood Arts 100 for late models by leading and finished up a winner after falling behind shortly after the start.

Shugart Zips To Feature $

BRUNSWICK, Ga.—Wayne Shugart captured the 99-lap "Hoo-Doo" Friday the 13th feature for late model stocks at Golden Isles Speedway.

For all but nine of the 99 laps, Shugart's Chevelle edged out first one and then another challenger for the $800 event. Early leader Rance Phillips spun on lap five but recovered and fought his way back to second spot where he remained until ten laps from the end when he was retired with a broken rod end. Phillips won the first

The 100-lap race on Atomic Speedway's 3/10-mile dirt track attracted 65 late models and 20 hobby stockers and a near capacity turnout of close to 5,000 despite bitter 46-degree weather.

Joe Lee Johnson overhauled Estes on the fourth lap and set the pace until Estes retook the lead on lap 31. From there on in it was the tootler all the way.

There were four makes of cars represented in the top finishers. Behind Estes' Chevelle were current point leader Snooks DeFoor in a Mustang; third went to Leroy Van in a Camaro and fourth money was collected by Clay Kelly in a Chevy II.

The prize fund totaled nearly $8,000. Johnson, after losing the lead, spun out and retired right at the 50-lap mark.

Other finishers in the century grind were: 5. Bob Ritchie, Camaro; 6. Otis

Miley, 7. Johnny Hogan, 8. Tex Gibson, 9. Bill Ogle, all driving Chevy IIs, and Amos Smith's Ford Fairlane was tenth in the 20-car field.

Ken Phillips, Camaro, won the 40-lap late model semi feature with the 30 lap consolation race honors to Wayne Montgomery. Mike Trentham won the 20-lap hobby feature.

Capital $ to Finish Is Pro

By ED WALLACE

WEST SACRAMENTO, Calif. — Mike Wasina, defending champion of the Supermodified Car Owners Assn., picked off his first main event victory of the season Saturday night on the quarter-mile clay oval at West Capital Raceway.

Masina started in ninth in

63

CHAPTER SEVEN

TOOTLE ESTES WINS HIS LAST RACE

The track known to both race fans and drivers as "The Gap" is actually the Volunteer Speedway located off I-81 in Bull's Gap, Tennessee. The 4/10th of a mile dirt oval first opened in mid-season of 1974. Over the years a number of dirt racing's best have been to victory lane at The Gap. They include, Scott Bloomquist, Herman Goddard, Vic Hill, H.E. Vineyard, Tommy Kerr, Buddy Rogers, L.D. Ottinger, Bill Corum, Danny Burks, Gusty Christenberry, Scott Sexton, Ronnie Johnson, Billy Ogle, Jr., Jimmy Owens, Ray Cook, Rusty Goddard and many others. One of those others was a Knoxville, Tennessee driver Herbert Estes, known to both his legions of race fans and fellow drivers as "Tootle" Estes.

In the 50 plus years of following this sport no other dirt track has played such a unique role in my memories of late model dirt racing as the Volunteer Speedway. My emotional spectrum has ran its course at this high banked East Tennessee racing facility.

On June 9, 1979 my happiest memory occurred, watching my long time friend, H.E. Vineyard win the NDRA "Looney Chevrolet 100" over racing great, Buck Simmons and a field of NDRA stars. On August 20, 1982, I experienced the

Estes powers by in the Curtis Equipment #199 race car Photo provided by Rocky Estes).

opposite end of the emotional spectrum. My saddest emotions occurred, as I learned that Tootle Estes, one of my all-time favorite drivers, had just had a massive heart attack and was pronounced dead at a local hospital. How could this be? I had just witnessed him winning a hard fought feature race and take the bounty money on Danny Burks a driver who seemed to own The Gap.

It had started out like any other racing Saturday night on a hot August day in the South. The fans started filing into the grandstands early and lay claim to the two or three top rows of seats, always the first to fill up. A short while later, as the water truck was putting some of the last water on the high banked dirt track, the drivers, with their varying types of haulers, started filling the pit area. One of those drivers was Tootle Estes, with his trademark bag of bubble gum and his duffle bag, containing his racing helmet and gear. Estes made his way over to his new #199 Curtis Equipment Firebird race car, parked in the one and two turn pit area, and talked with car owner Ralph Curtis and the rest of the crew.

Estes had been a regular at the nearby Newport Speedway for most of the season. However, he had wrecked his other race car at the Anderson (SC) Speedway recently and had missed several races at Newport. This cost him the points lead. So, Tootle had decided to race this particular Saturday night at "The Gap" because a driver by the name of Danny Burks had scored a number of wins recently and the track had put a "Bounty" on Burks for anyone who could beat him to the checkered flag.

As the drivers meeting was breaking up, the drivers and their crews made last minute adjustments to their racing machines. Hot laps, and heat races followed and then it was intermission. As the 40 lap late model feature approached, it was time to line up the cars and in a double file they took the green flag. The race was a crowd pleasing battle between Estes, Burks, Buddy Rogers, Bill Corum, L.D. Ottinger, and several other drivers. The whole 40 laps was a torrid battle up front between Estes, Burks, and several drivers. Estes worked hard the whole race, holding off several challenges for the lead. As the checkered flag came out, it was old Tootle who had scored the win and collected the bounty on Burks.

Everything appeared to be business as usual. Estes walked over to Ralph Curtis and thanked him, telling Ralph that he had, "Given me the best late model I have ever sat down in." Other drivers, including Ottinger, Rogers, and even Burks, along with several fans came by to congratulate Tootle on his win. Estes true to form, gave all the credit to car owner Curtis and his crew.

It was after a conversation with Drury Ramsey, owner of Newport Speedway, that Estes started talking about "how hard" the race car had been to steer during the race. Tootle began complaining about his arms hurting and began having a shortness of breath. If you knew Estes very long you knew he was always going on about some ache or pain, so everyone just took his complaints in stride.

However, it was fellow driver and longtime friend, Buddy Rogers that picked up on what was happening to Estes. Buddy recognized the telltale symptoms, it was a heart attack! Rogers quickly loaded Tootle into Estes' Ford Thunderbird, along with Tootle's wife, Barbara, and away they went up I-81 toward the Morristown-Hamblin Hospital. According to some, Rogers stopped the Ottinger crew and Jason Young got in the car to assist.

As they were speeding toward the hospital a tire blew out and several fans and drivers who had left the race track called for help on their C.B. Radios. It was a Pennsylvania registered nurse who answered the call. She administered cardiopulmonary resuscitation on the way to the hospital. However, Tootle Estes was pronounced dead shortly after arriving at the Hospital. It was said, his death was due to a massive heart attack.

In just a few short minutes, Tootle had gone from winning a hard fought race, to being pronounced dead due to a heart attack. The racing world had lost one of the true greats of Southern racing. Tootle Estes will forever be known as a pioneer in the sport; and as you have seen, one of the few drivers that was competitive in any type of race car that he ever strapped into. Tootle had ran his final race, and fittingly it was another checkered flag for, "The Little Engine That Could."

Racer Tootle Estes Dies Following Win

By Darlene Loveday
and Tom Sizemore

Herbert William (Tootle) Estes, 52, of Knoxville won his final race on August 20, when he finished first in the 40 lap late model feature at Volunteer Speedway in Bulls Gap to end a racing career that spanned over two decades on the dirt and asphalt tracks of the South.

The driver became ill in the pit after his victory and told several of his fellow drivers that his car had been hard to steer.

Buddy Rogers, an opponent and friend of the stricken driver put him in Estes' Thunderbird and began the race against time to Morristown-Hamblin Hospital.

Rogers stopped the L.D. Ottinger crew on Interstate 81 and Jason Young got in the car to assist them on the way. It was reported that Rogers was running in excess of 100 MPH when a tire blew out.

Several fans and drivers returning from the race got on C.B.'s and appealed for help and a registered nurse from Pennsylvania stopped and administered cardiopulmonary resuscitation, but Estes was pronounced dead on arrival at the hospital from an apparent heart attack.

Estes was a veteran driver who had tried almost all types of racers. He started in the old modified machines in the 1950's, was on the NASCAR briefly, and spent the last twelve years racing on dirt tracks.

Estes chalked up an estimated 1500 feature victories during his lengthy career. Atomic, Ashway and Knoxville were among the tracks where he captured season driving championships. He also gained state crowns in North Carolina, South Carolina, Georgia, Alabama and Tennessee.

His highest finish in a NASCAR Grand National race was tenth in the 1958 Southern 500 at Darlington. Later, he won many NASCAR late model sportsman events on such speedways as Daytona, Talladega and Charlotte.

Drury Ramsey, owner of the Newport Raceway, who talked with Estes after his Bulls Gap victory said, "It was just one of those freak things. I said something to him about winning the Late Model Feature at Bulls Gap, and he just laughed and said he wanted to give they guys who had worked on his car the credit. That's the kind of fella he was.

"He won a lot of races here (at Newport)," Ramsey continued. "He was running fifth in points to date, but was in first until wrecking his car at Anderson Speedway and had to miss several races while building a new car.

"You never met a nicer fella," said Ramsey. "He was always laughing and talking. He never gave any of the other drivers any trouble. Nobody ever protested Tottle. But if it came to a battle between

him and another guy, Tottle would back off and let the other guy go and settle for second.

"Nobody ever said anything bad about Tottle. Race fans liked him. Everybody liked him."

Fellow racer L.D. Ottinger said "I was never sure of a win when Tottle was in a race because he never quit challenging. He loved racing and he was as good a driver as I've ever competed against. I've lost a friend."

It was appropriate that Tootle Eastes would "go out in a blaze of glory." He was proud of his new number 199 Curtis Equipment Sales Firebird and although victory was nothing unique to Estes, he was always thrilled to be first under the checkered flag. He was loved by fans, friends and fellow drivers alike. He was well known for his sunny disposition and his willingness to talk with the fans.

When the Newport Raceway Flagsman, Burl Peters, lines up the dirt track racers to start the 40-lap Late Model Feature, engines will roar. Yet one engine will remain silent, but those dirt track racers will run as usual.

The crowd will cheer, the red dust will fly and the checkered flag will carry the winner around the high banked oval. Those who knew and loved Tootle Estes will remember that one is gone from among us but we'll be consoled by the fact that we knew a true

winner.

Estes is survived by his wife, Barbara and sons Rocky, Johnny, and Brian. Services will be held Monday at Mynatt's Funeral Home Chapel, with burial in Lynnhurst Cemetery in Knoxville.

Tootle Estes
with No. 199

CHAPTER EIGHT

TOOTLE ESTES
A TRUE DIRT RACING LEGEND

It was early on Saturday morning May 14, 2016 when I arrived for the Second Annual Banks County (GA) Speedway Reunion. The weather was perfect, not a cloud in the sky, as the race fans, drivers, and the vintage race cars started arriving. I had been working on my new book on the life of the Knoxville, Tennessee dirt racer, Herb "Tootle" Estes, trying to decide if Estes was indeed a true racing legend.

According to most definitions, a "legend" is a famous or important person who is known for doing something extremely well. I had almost decided that Tootle Estes fit this definition to a tee.

After this reunion all doubts about Tootle Estes being a racing legend were put to rest. As people started to show up, several people began telling me their memories of Estes' days of driving modifieds and skeeters throughout Northeast Georgia and South Carolina. Dewayne McCannon, a race fan I had been talking to on the subject of Estes, brought me a big folder of articles and newspaper clippings about Tootle. Even some of the relatives of the legendary dirt racer Buck Simmons like, Tim Simmons, Tina Simmons, and Parris Simmons came by and talked about their memories of Buck and Tootle. Tim told me, "I asked Buck one time who his mentor in racing was. And he said without hesitation, Tootle Estes."

He'd Race for 'Nothing'

Toodle Estes Gets His Hip-Pocket Money, Fun Driving Stock Cars

TOODLE ESTES
Covered 'em all

By BILL LUTHER

Racing on the Southeast's small dirt tracks isn't the most popular way to earn a livelihood — that is, unless your name is Toodle Estes.

Such has been the life of Estes for the past 13 years—driving on four and five tracks in as many nights and covering 900 miles on the road between races.

Since getting behind the wheel for the first time at old Broadway Speedway back in 1953, Toodle, whose given name is Herbert, has tackled most of the South's minor speedways and the toughest of them all—Darlington International Raceway.

The Knoxvillian has raced every type racer — stocks late model sportsmen, modified, super modified and jalopys, or hobby cars.

Estes, 35, the father of boys 9 and 12, is believed to be the only driver in this area relying entirely on racing for income.

"Jim Bradshaw and I split the winnings 50-50," said Estes. "I like racing so much I'd get me a job and race for nothing if I had to," said Toodle.

Bradshaw, of Anderson, S. C., owns two of the cars which Estes races. Today he and Bradshaw are in Georgia competing.

An ordinary week for Estes, during the summer months, runs something like this: Thursday at Greenwood, S. C.; Friday at Asheway Speedway; Saturday at Kingsport or Mobile, Ala.; Sunday afternoon at Tocooa, Ga.; and Saturday night at Cummings, Ga. He spends the remaining two or three days, which ever the case may be, playing golf at Whittle Springs or fishing on one of the area lakes.

Probably one of the biggest thrills for Estes came on Labor Day, 1958, when he ran 10th in the famed Southern 500 at Darlington, S. C.

Most of the races in which Estes competes pay $250-$500 to the feature winner. Toodle has had some big years, too. In 1956 he captured the feature event 64 times while driving in the late model sportsman division and in 1964 he ran feature 49 times in a modified.

This season he's running modified, late model sportsman and super modified.

How long does he plan to stay with such a grind?

"As long as I can," said Toodle. "I want to race for a long time . . . longer than I have."

"I suppose I've been lucky," he said. "I've been in many bad wrecks but hurt only once and burned twice when my car caught fire." His most serious injury came at Broadway Speedway where he suffered a fractured skull when his car flipped and the seat belt broke.

"It takes a rich man to race in NASCAR now unless you've got factory backing," said Estes. "I'd like to run the stocks if racing ever goes back to the independent."

Most competitive car? As far as Estes is concerned it's the super modified. They'll hit around 110 miles per hour on a half-mile dirt track such as Smoky Mountain Raceway at Maryville.

What about the nickname? "I didn't get it racing. I've had it all my life," said Toodle.

He'd race for nothing. (Article provided by Rocky Estes.)

Before I decided to write this book, I had heard many race fans and drivers alike over the years, tell me their memories of Estes. During the promotional tour of my two new books on late model dirt racing, I have traveled to a number of dirt tracks all over the Southeast including, Smoky Mountain Speedway, the Volunteer Speedway, Toccoa Speedway, Lavonia Speedway, Cherokee Speedway, and many others. Everywhere I have been race fans and drivers always talk fondly of their memories of Tootle and the many different types of race cars he drove.

Tootle was devoted to the sport of dirt racing throughout his career. He once said, "I always wanted to race and have been fortunate enough to make a living out of the sport I love." He went on to say, "I just get a thrill buckling into a race car and trying to beat the best drivers around. I also love traveling all over and competing on a lot of different tracks." In closing he said, "If I had to, I'd race for free, that's how much I love racing."

After writing this book, I have no doubt that Tootle Estes is a true racing legend. He started racing as a teenager and has successfully driven about every kind of race car that had four wheels during his long and successful career.

Estes was always a fair competitor, racing everyone hard for the win. In addition, he was a crowd favorite at about every track he raced. Finally, Tootle is a true racing legend for the simple fact that drivers and race fans alike still talk about him 34 years after he died; doing what he did best, winning a race. In closing I'll just say, myself and probably everyone else will always remember Herbert "Tootle" Estes as, "The Little Engine That Could."

BACK OF THE BOOK PHOTOS

An early H.E. Vineyard jalopy race car. Note the tow bar on the front. This is how they were towed to the races during this time period (Photo provided by David "Peanut" Jenkins).

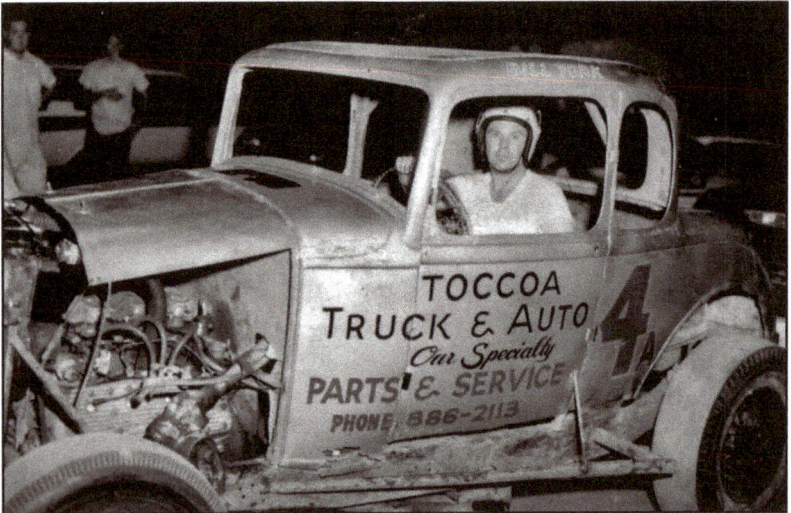

Georgia dirt warrior, Bill York sits in his Toccoa Truck and Auto jalopy race car (Photo provided by Brad York)

Gary L. Parker

Bill York being interviewed beside his jalopy race car shortly before a race (Photo provided by Brad York).

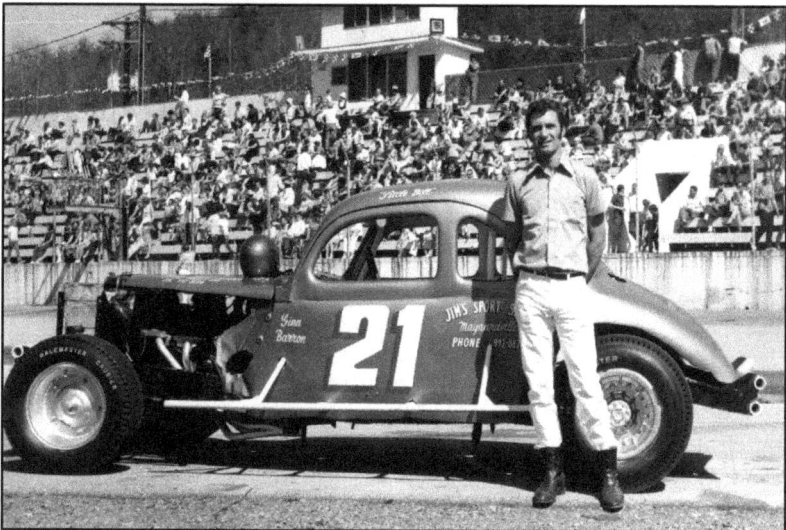

"Little" Bill Corum poses beside his modified race car at the Tazewell Speedway (Photo provided by Bill Corum).

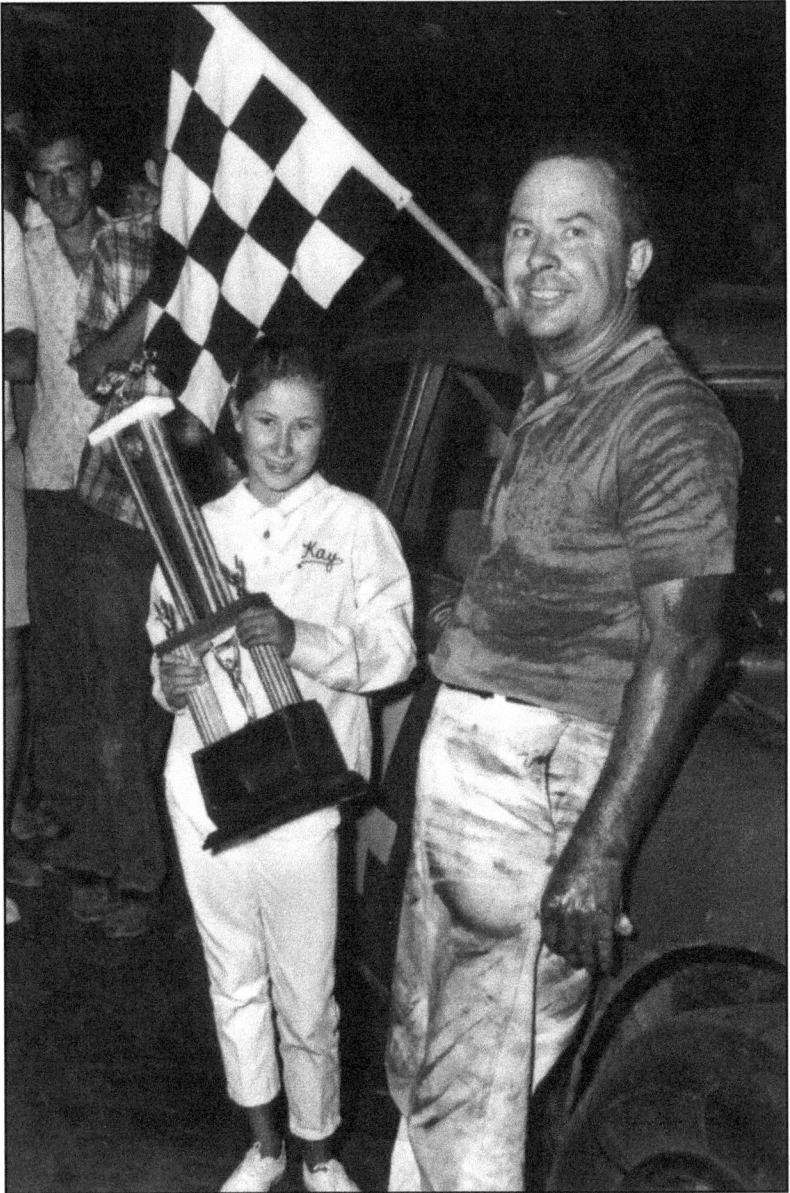

Georgia driver, Bill York accepts the trophy after winning a 200 lap sports-man race at the Anderson (SC) Speedway (Photo provided by Brad York).

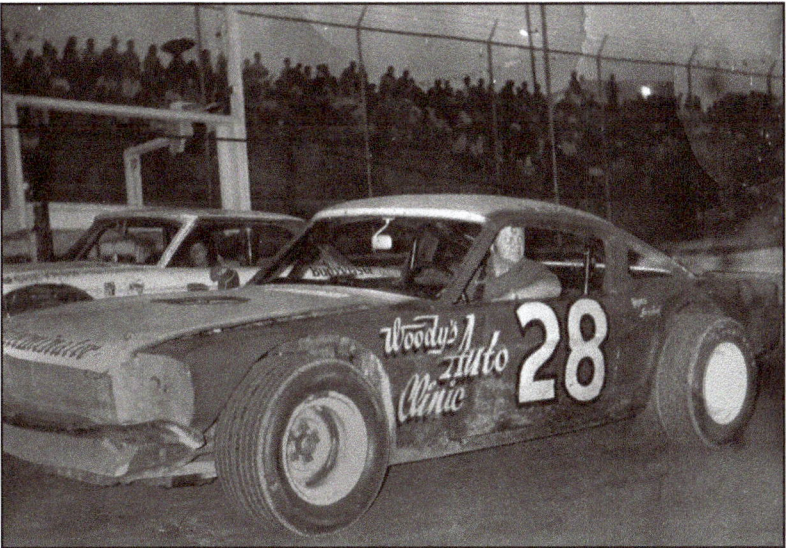

Tootle Estes in the Woody Bradley Ford Mustang (Photo provided by Wayne Wells).

My all time favorite race car. The Woody Bradley yellow #28 Ford Fairlane (Photo provided by Wayne Wells).

Tootle Estes' pit crew takes a break in the action at Smoky Mountain Speedway during the Summer of 1971. They are, Wayne Wells, Butch York, and car owner, Woody Bradley.

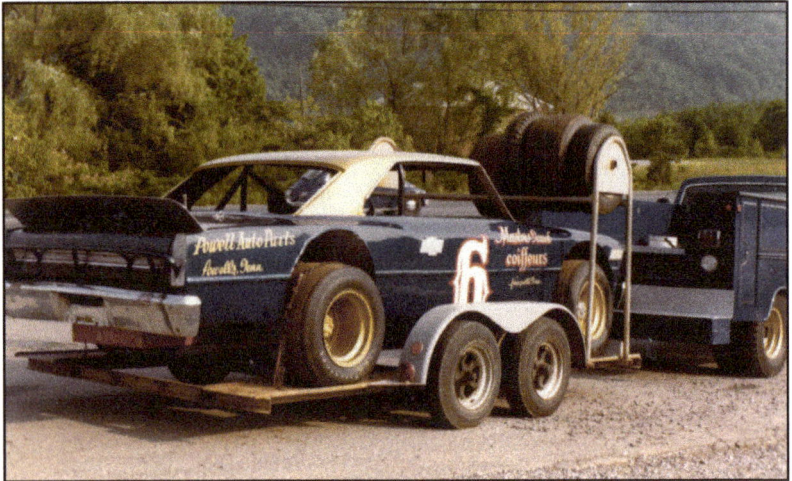

Tootle's #6 Chevy Nova loaded on the car hauler (Photo provided by Wayne Wells).

Estes posing beside the Danny Evans Masters Touch Coiffeurs #6 Chevy Nova (Photo provided by Wayne Wells).

Tootle's #6 Chevy Nova shortly before a race (Photo provided by Wayne Wells).

Tootle Estes preparing for hot laps at the historic Atomic (TN) Speedway (Photo provided by Wayne Wells).

The ever funny Tootle Estes enjoys a break in the racing action at Atomic (TN) Speedway. This photo was taken in the scoring tower as Tootle and another legendary driver, H.E. Vineyard, share a funny moment with a young lady (Photo provided by David "Peanut' Jenkins).

Gary L. Parker

The National Dirt Late Model Hall of Famer, Herbert "Tootle" Estes, "The Little Engine That Could" (Photo from an NDRA program and the Rocky Estes collection).

Myriad Pro and Souses on LSI #50 Archival white
Type and Design by Karen Paul Stone